# AN IMPOSSIBLE GOD

# An Impossible God

Frank Topping

**Hodder & Stoughton**
LONDON SYDNEY AUCKLAND

British Library Cataloguing in Publication Data
A record for this book is available from the British Library

ISBN 0 340 67121 1

Typeset by Hewer Text Composition Services, Edinburgh
Printed and bound in Great Britain by
Cox & Wyman Ltd, Reading, Berks.

Hodder and Stoughton Ltd
A Division of Hodder Headline PLC
338 Euston Road
London NW1 3BH

To June,
who enables me to dream

# Contents

Foreword by Maurice B. Copus, OBE      ix
Introduction      xi

I. An Impossible God      1

II. The Stations of the Cross      13
1. Jesus is Condemned to Death      17
2. Jesus Takes Up His Cross      21
3. Jesus Falls for the First Time      27
4. Jesus Meets His Mother      31
5. Simon Helps Jesus to Carry His Cross      34
6. Veronica Wipes the Face of Jesus      39
7. Jesus Falls for the Second Time      43
8. Jesus Speaks to the Women of Jerusalem      47
9. Jesus Falls for the Third Time      51
10. Jesus is Stripped of His Garments      55
11. Jesus is Nailed to the Cross      59
12. Jesus Dies on the Cross      64
13. Jesus is Taken Down from the Cross      69
14. Jesus is Placed in the Tomb      73

III. The Stations Beyond the Cross      77
1. Jesus Appears to Mary Magdalene      79
2. Jesus Appears at Emmaus      87
3. Jesus Appears to the Disciples      96
4. Jesus Appears to Thomas      101
5. Jesus Appears on the Beach at Galilee      108
6. Jesus Ascends into Heaven      120
7. The Disciples Receive the Holy Spirit      126

Bibliography      131

# Foreword

It gives me great pleasure to introduce this new edition of Frank Topping's *An Impossible God.*

I am Director of Group 81, the Diocesan Drama Company in Canterbury, which was founded in 1981 with the aim of encouraging the use of drama within the Church. Many plays and dramatic performances have been presented in repertory in the churches and cathedrals of Kent and on tour in Chichester, Exeter and Norwich. I fervently hope that drama will flourish in the Church and that it will play its part in communicating the Christian message.

I first read *An Impossible God* over ten years ago and I recognised that in the powerful writing of Frank Topping there exists a strong potential for dramatic presentation together with a deep spiritual integrity. Since then I have directed *An Impossible God* in nearly fifty churches and used sections in street presentations on Good Friday. In Dover, where actors played their parts from the back of a lorry, a large crowd followed it to various stations within the town. A participant wrote, 'It really brought the Passion home to me; everyone listened intently and it was a most moving experience.'

Frank presents the well-known facts of the Crucifixion from fresh angles with words that ask to be spoken, not read. His words are simple, telling and convincing; there is beauty in the writing, and he creates memorable phrases which come to mind again later, giving an excitement of recognition and at the truth of their meaning. I have worked so often with the piece that it could have become almost too familiar, but this is not so; as I rehearse it again the words are fresh and I discover new meanings and thoughts not apparent to me before.

*An Impossible God* has been well received by many audiences, some of whom have seen it as part of their preparation for Easter, and it has inspired those who have taken part. A player comments, 'The part of Martha had a deep effect on me. In one wonderful speech her bitterness with Jesus at Lazarus' death dissolves and turns into the most profound faith that He is who He says He is. All her resentment is wiped out by this revelation.' The person who recently played Peter, an actor of wide experience who has spent a lifetime as a Church Army evangelist, says, 'Frank Topping's writing encapsulates everything I have ever felt about Peter. I have been profoundly affected by the experience of playing the part and I long to do it again. Frank's words provide me with the ideal means of evangelism.'

Frank's words are good to speak; they hold the attention and many actors feel a strong rapport with their audience as they deliver the lines. As an actor himself Frank appreciates dramatic emphasis. The biblical characters come wonderfully alive, fleshed out with thought and deep feelings – you are really there in Jerusalem. A member of one audience wrote, 'Last night I simply could not stop to speak, I was just totally bowled over! The performance – everyone's – was so moving and so well done that any chit-chat would have seemed trivial.'

A vicar in whose church Group 81 performed *An Impossible God* commented, 'I was greatly impressed by the ability of the company to create such a powerful and deeply moving experience. I thought Frank Topping's work itself was most refreshing, especially in his extensive use of biblical material.'

*An Impossible God* holds a special place in the repertoire of Group 81. I am delighted that through this new edition more people will become familiar with the work of Frank Topping and with the message he seeks to spread.

Maurice B. Copus, OBE

# Introduction

In 1967 I had the good fortune to meet the Reverend F. Wesley Clifford. He was a retired Methodist minister who had spent many years of his ministry in India. He lived in a beautiful little Regency house in Brighton, in a hardly noticeable side street only yards from the sea. I have warm memories of descending the narrow stairs to the basement room where he had established his study. I remember a comfortable room, book-lined from floor to ceiling, his desk at the window facing the small back garden, a pair of easy chairs before a blazing fire, tea and conversation that was still alive as daylight faded and the flickering fire cast huge and distorted shadows.

He was a tall, white-haired man, and the smallness of his house made him seem taller. A considerable scholar, he kept up to date with the latest trends in theological thought and discussed them with the tolerance of well-read age. He was also a deeply spiritual man whose patience and generosity both put me to shame and delighted and encouraged me at the same time. He used to call me "Old Warrior", a term of address that I borrowed and gave to the Revd Walter Spoonbill, in *God Bless You, Spoonbill*.

One late winter's afternoon he introduced me to a book which he said he had read every Lent for years. It was *The Passion and Death of Our Lord Jesus Christ*, by Archbishop Alban Goodier S.J., published by Burns Oates in 1933. It is a fascinating study of the Passion which recreates the thoughts and arguments of the time, brings vividly to mind the streets of New Testament Jerusalem, the sounds of the traders and the smell and breath of their animals. The book was precious to Wesley Clifford, and although he offered to lend it to me, I would not dream of borrowing it.

A few weeks later, sitting by Wesley Clifford's fire, he produced, like a conjurer, a second copy of Archbishop Goodier's book, a triumphant "find" in a second-hand bookshop in the "Lanes" in Brighton. "It's for you, Old Warrior, a gift."

I owe a great debt to Archbishop Goodier's book, and feel now that I know him quite well. Not surprisingly I cannot agree with everything that he says. Since he wrote his book modern scholarship has advanced by leaps and bounds in the examination of the source material of the texts, and of the texts themselves. The Archbishop however was less concerned with this form of criticism. He was concerned, as he says, with questions about the person of Christ. "How does the Passion reveal Christ to us?", "What manner of man does he show himself to be during that ordeal?", "What were his thoughts and feelings?" In this area the Gospels are silent and scholarship can only be conjectural. I suspect that were the Archbishop to be presented with the findings of the most up-to-date criticism, his book would not need to be altered to any great extent. His insight comes more from an understanding of love, pain, compassion and human frailty.

To imagine what someone was thinking centuries ago can only be conjecture, and no two scholars would agree on every point, but with the help of a variety of modern commentators and of course Archbishop Goodier, I can only hope that my conjecture is not so much "wild" as "informed". Although I have tried to be as accurate as possible about physical details, the topography of Jerusalem in New Testament times is as debatable as are the shades of meaning in the texts. Nevertheless I am deeply indebted and grateful for the work of the commentators, for the inspiration of Archbishop Goodier and not the least to the guiding hand of Wesley Clifford.

# I.  An Impossible God

# An Impossible God

It seems to me that the radical Christian wants a God that will comply with current, rational, scientific thought. He wants an intellectually respectable God, a "possible" God.

The Christian fundamentalist, for different reasons, also wants a God that can be contained within a formula. He wants an orderly system of life with infallible rules based on an infallible Bible. There is then no need for argument if "the Bible tells me so" becomes the literal authority for all thought and action.

In other words I think the fundamentalist reduces argument to absurdity, whilst the radical reduces God to absurdity.

I say this from the giddy intellectual and spiritual height of someone who knows himself to be capable of embracing both fundamentalist and radical views at one and the same time.

"The Bible tells me so" is a statement that can make me smile sadly in one context and nod in agreement in another.

There are also times when the whole idea of a God, a creative, reasoning God, who is in any way aware of mankind, let alone me, seems a ludicrously childlike dream, mere wishful thinking.

James Thurber's moral tale of "The bear who could take it or leave it alone", in which the drunkard's strength is compared with the excesses of the physical fitness fanatic, highlights, as only a humorist can, the truth of the saying "You might as well fall flat on your face as lean too far backwards." I have referred to two extremes; there are, of course, other approaches, between the extremes. I am thinking of those mystics and saints who appear to have transcended theological argument by the quality of their lives. Perhaps they are even more extreme in a totally different direction. They are usually sane, ordinary people made extraordinary by their commitment to an impossible love revealed by an impossible God.

I have been trying to understand the experience of those sane, ordinary people in the New Testament who were confronted by the impossible God.

The idea of an impossible God sounds paradoxical, but a definable God, a possible God, is more of a contradiction in terms. God ceases to be God if he can be reduced to any form of definition. God cannot be limited by human reasoning. The infinite cannot be encompassed by the finite, except that that is precisely what God does in Christ. The God-man figure is, in our terms, impossible.

It is no easier to attempt to say what the impossible God is *not* than what he *is*. For instance, it could be said that to ascribe gender to God is nonsense, an anthropomorphic limitation, yet Jesus taught us to say "Our Father". "He" and "She" both present problems as terms of reference for God, but they are more appropriate than "it", which removes personality altogether.

Jesus the man was limited by language and historical environment, but what words could Jesus, the God-man, have used to describe something outside of human experience? If "Father" was the nearest he could get, how can I argue? On the other hand, who Jesus is, is more important than what he said. St John says that he was "the Word made flesh". I remember William Barclay once suggesting that it is a useful exercise to consider "the Word" as "the mind of God", which provides an interesting view of the opening verses of St John's Gospel:

> In the beginning was the mind of
> God . . . and the mind of God became flesh
> and dwelt among us.

4

Limited and unlimited, that is the paradox of our impossible God: the God of all creation, beyond the universe, omnipresent and living in Nazareth learning carpentry.

The dilemma about the nature of God is not exactly new, even though recent newspaper articles and television programmes have referred to "the current crisis of faith". One wonders what fevered debate took place before the psalmist rushed home, and making his own position absolutely clear, wrote, "The fool in his heart says there is no God" (Psalm 14; cf. Psalm 53). I once mused over this text as it applied to me, and it is from this "musing" that I took the title of ". . . an impossible God".

> The fool in his heart says,
> "There is no God."
> He is no simpleton, this fool,
> on the contrary, he is clever,
> too clever for God.
> And I know this cleverness;
> I know the questions, the doubts,
> the panic that asks,
> "Is there anybody there –
> am I fooling myself?
> Is it all a trick of the mind?"
>
> Am I afraid of the idea
> of a God who is a person?
> Would I rather have the rationalist's God,
> some amorphous intelligence,
> the cause of an evolutionary system,
> impersonal, detached, disinterested;
> a theory, bloodless, gutless,
> without mystery – a possible God?
> If that is the sane, rational concept of God
> then I prefer the insanity of faith
> in a God who is not removed from his creation
> but part of it.

5

A God who understands
anguish, laughter,
birth and death.
I am not given meaning, redeemed,
by a theory.
I am redeemed
by a weeping, forgiving,
loving, dying God.
Not a God who exists somewhere
on the outer fringe of an infinite universe,
but a God
born in a stable,
hung on a cross
and alive in my world, my life;
a rollicking, tragic mystery,
an impossible God.

Where is the wise man?
Where is the debater of this age?
Has not God made foolish
the wisdom of the world,
for the foolishness of God
is wiser than men.
The fool in his heart says,
"There is no God."
And the Lord looks down from heaven
upon the children of men
to see if there are any
that act wisely,
any, that seek God.

I am not a systematic theologian, but an extremely
unsystematic pilgrim whose reason seeks answers to
experience; who has found that his reason limits his
exploration, and wishes, not unreasonably, to go beyond
reason.

What lies beyond reason – insanity, divinity, a void? I

am not brave enough to leap wholeheartedly into that terrifying space, as I believe those extraordinary people, the saints, have done. I have merely waggled my toes over the edge whilst clinging fiercely to the apparent terra firma of "sense". My explorations into the world of the impossible God consist of the feeble and inadequate prayers of a child who is afraid of the dark. When I approach the edge of this great divide I have the desire to go further but my courage wavers. I am like some would-be loyal friend of Christopher Columbus, who trusts his friend but fears that they might yet fall off the edge of the world.

Many of us, brought up in Christian families nurtured in the Christian faith, have experienced this profound doubt. We have felt that awful sinking feeling, a black panic in which we have asked ourselves, "Is there anything there? Is it all a trick of the mind? Perhaps there is no God?" I suspect that questions like these were racing through the minds of those gathered in the upper room the morning after the death of Christ.

The story of Jesus Christ is told by ordinary men and women. The telling of the story reveals their own doubts, inadequacies and lack of certainty about Jesus. When Christ is executed they are totally depressed, confused and frightened. The great game is over. It is rapidly becoming a memory of a wild dream that went disastrously wrong. Therefore they decide to behave sensibly; keep quiet, deny any association with Jesus, and lie low.

After the crucifixion, when the first report of Christ's rising from the dead was brought to the disciples, they totally dismissed the story as impossible. Mary Magdalene was not believed. Thomas vehemently demands proof and will not tolerate the story even from his closest friends.

But those sane, rational unbelievers subsequently tell us that they were confronted by an impossible fact. How do you describe an impossible fact? Of more importance, what do you do about it? What do you do with the rest of your life? Nobody dies for an improbable theory,

7

yet most of those who witnessed the risen Christ laid down their lives declaring the impossible fact, that they had met, talked and eaten with a man who had come back from the dead. It was not a question of casting aside their doubts and believing, they were required to cast aside their convictions and believe. They were not primarily theologians. They did indeed want to persuade and convince; this they did, principally by declaring what had happened to them. Paul, of course, was a theologian, and being a theologian he could not resist attempting to express his Christian theology. At the Areopagus in Athens, Paul tried to persuade the Epicurean and Stoic philosophers with a theological argument. He was not totally unsuccessful, but the experience made him decide that in the future he would simply declare the *fact* of the risen Christ. In his first letter to the Corinthians (chapter 15) Paul says –

> Now I would remind you, brethren, in what terms I preached to you the Gospel . . . For I delivered to you as of first importance what I also received, that Christ died for our sins in accordance with the scriptures and that he appeared to Cephas, then to the twelve. Then he appeared to more than five hundred brethren at one time . . . Then he appeared to James, then to all the apostles. Last of all, as to one untimely born, he appeared also to me.

He is speaking of those who had witnessed the impossible events. He is declaring experiences. The great analytical psychologist, Jung, echoed the first disciples when he said, "I do not need to believe, I know." Like the man, blind from birth, who in argument with the Pharisees about the nature of Jesus, said, "I don't know if he is a prophet. I know only one thing, I was blind, but now I see." His sight was a fact. The fact of an experience of Christ transcends all argument. I may not agree with the theology of Francis

8

of Assisi, or Mother Teresa of Calcutta, but I see in such people lives that have been transformed by their experience of Christ. They may not be able to prove their experience of Christ, but to them, as it was to the first disciples, the experience of Christ is a fact. They do not need to believe, they know!

The resurrection is indeed a stumbling block, it demands that we accept that which rational and scientific analysis declares to be impossible. However, when we look at the lives of those who have experienced the risen Christ, we do not see raving lunatics, we see lives so transformed, so filled with love, that the transformation takes our breath away. I am drawn towards such people and at the same time they terrify me because, standing on the shores of reason I fear that I will not be able to resist the invitation to walk on the sea of faith, to follow the impossible God to heaven knows where.

I find myself returning to the New Testament account of the Passion and resurrection, not merely to remind myself of the story, but in an attempt to hear the voices of the first witnesses; to understand their thoughts, to come closer, in fear and trepidation, to an experience of the risen Christ for myself.

I have found that it is not really possible to understand the resurrection stories apart from the Passion. The attack on reason, the shock of the resurrection stories, depends on a knowledge of the terrible reality of the Passion.

These pages are not arguments, they are inadequate and ill-expressed devotional thoughts. Also, I write from more than a committed position. I may only have my toes over the edge, but I know that I cannot turn back.

The meditations on the Passion follow a traditional form of devotion known as "The Stations of the Cross". I have followed a similar pattern with the post-resurrection events, which I have called "The Stations Beyond the Cross". In trying to understand the experience of those who witnessed the New Testament story I have attempted to see the events through their eyes. Because of this the book is not so much an argument as a kind of devotional reverie.

Apart from the Gospel quotations, all the speeches are, of course, imaginary. Some of the characters are imaginary and some are based on mere shreds of evidence. Such evidence could be interpreted in a variety of different ways, as for instance with the characters Simon of Cyrene and Veronica. I have included here some notes on Simon and Veronica to indicate at least how I have interpreted the evidence.

### Simon of Cyrene

All that is known of Simon is that he was the father of Alexander and Rufus. The fact that his sons are named in the Gospel (Mark 15:21) indicates that they were known to the early Church. In Paul's letter to the Romans (16:13) Paul says, "Greet Rufus, elect in the Lord, also his mother and mine", suggesting that he was well known to Rufus whose mother he counts as his own. (This was a customary oriental courtesy towards older women held in respect.)

There is no direct evidence that Paul's Rufus was the son of Simon of Cyrene. The circumstantial evidence is that the Gospel of Mark was probably written in Rome and therefore it is possible that the Rufus Paul greets in Rome is the same Rufus able to supply details to the Gospel writer.

Rufus is a Latin name, frequently given to slaves or freedmen. Because of this it has often been assumed that Simon of Cyrene was himself a freed slave, and this was the reason for the Roman soldiers choosing him as the one to be compelled into service. This is not necessarily the case. Not everyone called Rufus was, or had been, a slave, and the Romans could compel anyone they chose in a subject country. They are likely to have exercised a political tact on the eve of a great Jewish festival. For a Jew to be involved in the execution would have meant a ritual uncleanliness which would have been deeply shameful. A non-Jewish foreigner would therefore cause the least trouble.

We can only speculate, using such historical evidence as will support our theories. The Gospel simply refers to Simon as "a passerby from the country". Being from Cyrene tells us that he had, at some time, travelled very great distances. Cyrene is about a thousand miles from Jerusalem.

The fact that he and his sons are named, and the strong possibility that Rufus and his mother are the same family, active and well known in the early Church, suggests that the experience changed Simon from being a "passerby" to a disciple.


### Veronica

Veronica is a legendary figure. The legend, thought to be of French origin, emerged in its present form in the fourteenth century, and describes Veronica as a woman of Jerusalem who offered her headcloth to Jesus to wipe the blood and sweat from his face on the way to Calvary. When he returned the cloth to her, the legend says, his image was imprinted on it.

In the fourth and fifth century work *The Acts of Pilate*, there is an account of the healing of the woman suffering from "an issue of blood" (Mark 5:25–34). In *The Acts of Pilate* the woman is called Veronica. This book then tells a story in which Veronica is said to have cured the Emperor Tiberius with a miraculous portrait of Christ.

A twelfth century historian, Giraldus Cambrensis, Gerald de Barri (1147–c.1223) of Pembrokeshire, tells a story of a woman who, longing to see Christ, had sent him a headcloth, and when it was returned to her his features were impressed upon it. He refers to the cloth as the "vera εικωτ", that is, "true icon". "Vera icon" suggests that the name Veronica stems from a description of an image of Christ.

11

St Veronica is not mentioned in the Roman martyrology, but her feast is kept on 12th July.

Despite the lack of evidence, scriptural or otherwise, to support the identity or existence of Veronica, the story attributing the name to the woman healed by Jesus (who would very likely have become a devoted follower of Christ) has become an innocent means of meditating on a particular aspect of Christ's suffering and is entirely appropriate in a devotional exercise centred on the Passion. It is also in keeping with the historical account of the prominent part that women played in Christ's Passion.

# II.   The Stations of the Cross

# The Stations of the Cross

The Stations of the Cross is a devotional excercise practised throughout the year but especially at Lent and Passiontide. There is evidence, from a very early date, that Christian pilgrims to Jerusalem made a practice of following the traditional route taken by Jesus from the house of the Roman governor, Pontius Pilate, to Calvary and ultimately to the tomb in which Jesus was laid. As they made this journey they would stop and recall particular incidents in the Passion at various places along the route and pray and meditate on the sufferings of Christ.

Today, modern pilgrims find the stations marked, carved in stone tablets, along the Via Dolorosa within the old walled city of Jerusalem. Each station refers to an event such as when Jesus fell as he carried his cross, when he spoke to the women of Jerusalem and when Simon of Cyrene was compelled to help carry the cross. The path winds through the *suk*, the shops and stalls of Arab street traders which seem to have changed hardly at all in two thousand years. The Via Dolorosa ends and the final station is found at the tomb within the church of the Holy Sepulchre.

The devotional liturgy of the Stations of the Cross practised in European churches probably developed as a result of the early pilgrims returning home from Jerusalem and wanting to reproduce the intensity of their Via Dolorosa experience. In the later Middle Ages the devotion was popularised particularly by the Franciscans, but the selection of the Passion incidents to be included in the stations was not finally decided until the eighteenth or nineteenth century. Alphonso Di Liguri, the founder of the Redemptorist Fathers, is thought to have drawn up the definitive list of fourteen events or stations, and it is these stations that are included in this book.

In churches where this devotion is practised a series of

sculptures or paintings is arranged around the church walls. Priest and people process from one station to another, praying and meditating on the event associated with each station. In this book, as we follow in the steps of Jesus along the Via Dolorosa, we hear the thoughts of the people involved in or witnessing the original events and their reflections on earlier experiences in the life of Christ. After each voice has spoken there is a meditative prayer which links us with the original event and the world in which we live. The Stations of the Cross deal with the Passion and death of Jesus – but I have added a further seven stations which take us into the events which follow the Passion, and I have called them the Stations Beyond the Cross. At each station there will be short introductory notes.

Those who plotted the death of Jesus were beset by a number of problems. When Jesus entered Jerusalem on Palm Sunday his popularity among the ordinary people threw the city into an uproar (Matt. 21:10). The plotters could not make a move to arrest Jesus in daylight for fear of the reaction of the people.

A further difficulty lay in the fact that the death penalty could only be awarded and carried out for offences against Roman law and through a Roman court. The Romans were not interested in adjudicating in the theological contentions of local religions. Jesus had to be charged with an offence against Caesar, such as insurrection or treason. Jesus had always confounded attempts to make him speak against Roman rule in public, therefore charges against him could be achieved only by false accusation and false witnesses. Such charges failed to convince the Roman governor. Yet merely for the sake of quietening an incident that might have turned into an ugly riot, Pontius Pilate made a show of saying that he washed his hands of the affair, but nevertheless gave permission for an execution to be carried out and, in so doing, set in motion the most famous miscarriage of justice in history.

# 1. Jesus is Condemned to Death

## i.

*A servant of the High Priest*

It was quiet, unnaturally quiet.
Moon-sharpened shadows, weirdly shaped,
quickened the pulse
as we shivered in the stillness.
So still was it,
that the whimper of a restless child,
somewhere in the city,
startled us,
held us staring, breathless,
until the clicks of the sleepless crickets
reassured us that our vigil
had not been disturbed.

An hour,
at least an hour had passed
since he had entered the garden.
A torch flared,
Iscariot shielded his eyes
and then they moved,
furtive as sin,
through the olive trees
whispering behind the zealot.
We waited,
afraid and impatient.
It was for the best, we said.
But the very hour condemned,
the clandestine hour.

Even without the talk
of bribes and conspiracy
the night was heavy with treachery
and guilt.

We were afraid,
even in the virtuous safety
of the Sanhedrin.
It took courage
to lay hands on the man
who summoned Lazarus
from his tomb.
We were afraid,
of his silence,
more awesome,
more chilling,
more poignant than any pleading.
Through all the noise.
the shouting, the groaning,
the tearing of cloth,
so still was he,
so compelling,
that occasionally,
the raising of his eye-lids
silenced us.
And filled us
with fearful expectancy.

"Ecce homo!" Pilate shouted
and he was afraid,
indecision twitching his mouth,
Roman curls sweat-plastered to his brow
even with the sun not yet above the Temple.
And he trembled
in the long shadow of his wife
and longer shadow of his Caesar.
It was as if a shadow

18

had fallen across the people,
reducing the light to a dirty saffron;
a fleeting, patchy shadow
moving so swiftly that faces dissembled,
bodies merged,
became one shifting mass.
There was a pungent, evil odour,
as if shimmering from Hades
some sin-bewitched, satanic sleight of hand
had coalesced our eyes and mouths
into one bilious, pain-pinched face,
one distorted voice
that screeched with ageless malice,
"Crucify him!"

ii.

*Who condemns?*
*Jewish courts?*
*Roman governors?*
*"Look at the man!" he said,*
*but I cannot.*
*Adam's sin pivots the soul,*
*turns the brain,*
*turns my eyes*
*away from goodness,*
*away from love,*
*away from Christ,*
*until in sin's insanity*
*an inner voice shouts*
*"Away with him!*
*Give me what I want!*
*Give me Barabbas!"*

*Who condemns?*
*Not Caiaphas,*

not Pontius Pilate.
I know who condemns,
I know who snaps shut
the manacles of malice.
Christ is shackled
by greed-heated,
hate-hammered,
pride-forged chain;
by every thought, word and deed
that has ever offended love.

Who condemns?
A voice in the crowd cries out.
A voice I have heard
in arguments and rows,
distorted with anger and self-centred bitterness;
all the back-biting of years
contracted to two words
hissed through clenched teeth,
"Crucify him!"

My Lord and my God,
defeat me and forgive me.
Defeat my bitterness
with your peace.
Defeat my sin
with your love.

Having been sentenced to the barbarous death of a criminal, death by crucifixion, Jesus now begins the grim ritual of the condemned, the enforced carrying of the crossbeam to the place of execution. Historians have confirmed that it was common for condemned men to carry the transverse beam of a crucifixion cross rather than the whole structure; but as flogging usually preceded a crucifixion the crossbeam was burden enough.

## 2. Jesus Takes Up His Cross

### i.

*A maid in the house of Caiaphas*

I knew him, you see,
the man from Kerioth, Judas.
Knew him when he was a boy.
Talk about a trouble-maker!
Into everything he was,
gangs, fighting.
Patriots they called themselves.
The moment I saw him
I knew there would be trouble.
I wouldn't like to tell you
the things he's been mixed up with.
Must have broken his mother's heart
– poor woman.
A bit touched, if you ask me,
you could see it in his eyes.
Anyway, those were the instructions
– a man from Kerioth would call.

I didn't see him cross the yard,
and his knock didn't sound
like a knock,
more like scratching,
like a rat in the rafters.
Gave me quite a turn, he did.
I opened the shutter
and there he was,
staring through the bars
with his mad eyes.

And that was the start of it,
comings and goings all night.
And that poor man, Jesus,
pushing him about, hitting him.
Do you know? – I still don't know
what they had against him.
And they didn't know, either,
what to do with him.
They took him to old Annas first,
Ruth told me,
that's when they started hitting him.
Then they swarmed into our courtyard.
You'd think it was the middle of the day,
like a party, the noise, the shouting.
They took him in to Caiaphas.
Over two hours they were,
questioning him, shouting at him.
I asked one of the guards,
"What are they doing?"
"Trying him", he said.
"You can't try a man", I said,
"in the middle of the night,
even I know that!"
"Hold your tongue, woman!" he said.

Of course you can't talk to anybody nowadays.
I saw one of his friends, here in the courtyard,

22

all I said was, "You're one of his friends aren't
  you?"
Well, you'd think I'd accused him of murder.
"Me?" he said. "Not me, nothing to do with me."
"You sound like a Galilean", I said.
Nearly bit my head off he did.
"I tell you. I don't know the man!"
About an hour later,
one of the men who'd come in,
the one who lit the charcoal, he said,
"Didn't I see you down in the garden?"
I thought the Galilean was on the verge of tears.
"I tell you, I do not know the man!" he said.
Well, shouted really.
And then they brought him out,
Jesus, the prisoner.
We didn't get much sleep that night,
because the cock was crowing then,
that's how late it was.
I'd no sooner got my head down
than we were up.
The prisoner was in with Caiaphas again.
Then they marched him to the Governor's Hall,
and Pilate sends him to Herod's Palace
and Herod has his fun
and sends him back to Pilate.
That makes six trials, by my count,
two in the night and four in the morning.
Well, what do you have to do
to get six trials,
in the space of twelve hours?
That's what I'd like to know.

When I saw him next,
Jesus, the carpenter,
I couldn't believe it,
I could have cried

– well, I did.
Terrible sight he was.
God knows what they'd done to him.
His face, all bruised and bleeding.

They'd pushed some of those big thorns
right into his head, a ring of them,
like a crown.
And they'd flogged him,
he could hardly stand,
but he still looked a better man
than any in that crowd,
spitting, jeering, pushing
and laughing, horrible it was.
And they weren't drunk,
they hadn't even that excuse,
possessed, more like it,
that's what I think.

They lifted up the big plank.
I knew what it was.
I thought, Dear God,
he'll never carry that,
there's hardly any flesh on his back,
they'll kill him before he gets there.
Well, that would have been a mercy.
As God is my judge, I still don't know
what they had against him!
He wasn't a murderer.
He wasn't a villain.
He wasn't a thief.
A religious carpenter,
that's what he was,
and they let Barabbas go,
Barabbas!
I sometimes think
the world's gone mad.

## ii.

*How heavy*
*the cross of Christ.*
*No ordinary load*
*presses down on these shoulders.*
*How heavy is oppression?*
*How burdensome greed?*
*How distended envy?*
*How distorted and hard to hold*
*is the weight of centuries*
*of obscenity and cruelty?*
*No ordinary burden weighs*
*on this inlaid timber,*
*drilled*
*and filled*
*with the leaden weight of evil.*
*The murdered dead*
*and the wastes of war*
*increase its density.*
*Diseased, ruined lives*
*clamour for justice,*
*the sick and suffering*
*to the ends of time*
*cling to its corners.*

*"He was despised and rejected by men,*
*a man of sorrows, and acquainted with grief.*
*. . . Surely he has borne our griefs*
*and carried our sorrows.*
*. . . wounded for our transgressions,*
*. . . bruised for our iniquities.*
*. . . the Lord has laid on him*
*the iniquity of us all."*

*Behold the Lamb of God*
*who takes away,*

who bears,
who carries
the sins of the world.

Come to me
all you who are heavy laden
and I will give you rest,
for my yoke is easy
and my burden is light.

Lord.
You lift from me
the guilt, fear and regret
of years,
and in its place
your gentle yoke, even when resisted,
changes me.
I do not understand suffering.
In the isolation of your agony,
is your burden eased
by acts of love,
by sacrificial lives?
Is your burden shared
by the suffering
of the hungry and the sick?
Lord,
in spite of my fear,
in spite of the ease with which I declare,
"I do not know the man!"
Implant in me the courage
to make some sacrifice,
somewhere in my life
that might lighten,
by an infinitesimal fraction
the weight of your cross.

There is no scriptural reference to Jesus falling, but following the physical abuse he had already received and the continued mockery and violent jostling it is more than likely that he fell several times during that dreadful climb to Calvary.

## 3. Jesus Falls for the First Time

### i.

*A Scribe*

It was for the best, we said.
Better that one man should die
than many.
But how can the death of the innocent
improve the common good?
We knew the fear
of insurrection's penalty.
Judas the Gaulonite taught us that.
His rising was quelled
with a mile of crucified bodies
to remind us of the might of Rome.
But we knew that in truth,
a truth we dare not utter,
this man did not threaten Rome,
he threatened us.
He threatened Caiaphas, Annas,
scribes, priests and pharisees,
hypocrisy, pride, sham religion.
And how sharp
was the sting of his truth.
Woe unto you, scribes and pharisees,
hypocrites! White-washed sepulchres!
Clean on the outside and rotten within!

27

He ridiculed our fasting and almsgiving.
Challenged ceremony and rites,
criticized even our manner of prayer,
called us,
"A wicked and adulterous generation!"
In the Temple itself
to our faces, for all the world to hear,
he had accused,
"You have made my Father's house
a den of thieves."
From those same Temple stones
he had declared, before the people,
that we were degenerate sons of Abraham,
that the devil was our father!
He had even prophesied
that harlots, publicans and tax-gatherers
would enter the Kingdom before us,
that we would die in our sins
and that foreigners, gentiles,
rather than the tribe of Abraham,
would go before us into the Kingdom.
Before us,
priests and High Priests
of the sacred trust of Israel,
keepers and protectors
of the law of Moses,
covenanters with God,
*us*, he threatened *us*.
Not a word about military occupation,
not a word about patriotism,
no, he did not threaten Caesar,
but centuries of thought,
customs, laws, values,
religion itself.
He threatened all of us.
He had pricked the bladder of human wisdom
and then, inexplicably, stood in silence

as its bile spewed over him;
in silence, even when a murderer was chosen
as more worthy of life than he.
On the steps of Antonia's Castle,
bloodily crowned,
a royal cloak about his shoulders,
his presence was awesome.
Those of us who had seen him
parry and thrust with lawyers,
command the lame to stand,
outface angry mobs
and pass through their midst, unharmed,
we were held,
fascinated by his latent power,
aware that he had only to decide . . .
Then I saw, quite clearly,
he had not been cowed into submission.
He had chosen it.

There was pain
when they ripped away the cloak,
cut the cords that bound his hands
and threw his garment to him,
but pain that had been born
many years before.
Whatever it housed
it was still a human frame
with all its limitations.
Not a massive frame,
but average, slight,
probably underfed.
Both executioners grunted and cursed
beneath the burden of the crossbeam,
and spat with relief
when its weight was transferred.

Within the shadow of the Temple he fell,
one hundred paces from Pilate's feet,

and we were not surprised.
Yet some felt, surging through their veins,
not shock, but that more permanent sensation,
shame.

ii.

Lord.
*You stumble and fall*
*and I watch, appalled*
*as you multiply,*
*as a group of you stare at me,*
*large-eyed and starving.*
*I cannot believe what I see,*
*rib-taut hunger accuses me,*
*pot-bellied children*
*deep in the blank-eyed hollow of despair*
*ignore me.*
*And there you lie,*
*and there,*
*condemned to life*
*in a corrugated, cardboard,*
*polythene prison.*
*You stumble and fall*
*at the feet of the rich,*
*and deeply distressed,*
*I throw you a crumb.*

The meeting of Jesus and his mother while he carried the cross is not recorded in the scriptures. However, her presence is not only recorded but Jesus's concern for his mother is expressed directly to her from the cross. There is no doubt that she followed him on that terrible walk and there is no doubt that their eyes would have met.

## 4. Jesus Meets His Mother

i.

*John*

She did not speak,
did not weep,
did not touch,
but they met.
In the lane
from the Damascus Gate
dealers touted custom,
money-changers eyed travellers,
assessing their worth, wary.
The air,
thick with aromas,
spices, meat on spits,
animals and people,
and noise,
hooves and hammers
clanking, clinking,
clucking, bleating,
soldiers joking,
women, children,
shouting, laughing.

31

In the midst of babble
they met,
in a pocket
of love-charged silence.

All her life
she had searched for him,
the child she held
but could not hold,
the elusive core of him
beyond her reach.
But now,
in one long look
the years compressed,
from cradle to Egypt,
from carpentry
to Hosannas on a donkey,
Simeon's sword sinking deeper
and yet
she was nearer now
than she had ever been.

The mystery of his birth,
the mystery of his being
touched her, embraced her
into the mystery of his death.

When tears came
they did not reproach,
neither was there question
in her pain.
In the din
of money and men,
alone with him
her silence said,
"Behold the handmaid of the Lord."

## ii.

Mary, Mary,
mother of the manger child,
the temple boy,
the healing man,
by love's sacrifice
your heart is pierced,
by love's generosity
you are emptied.

Mary,
keeper of the secret
of the power
that enabled you to stand
before the child of your dreams
and walk with him
to sin's bitter triumph.

Mary,
in temptation
may we imitate your obedience.
When truth
becomes the butt of mockery,
may we possess your loyalty.
In the hour of trial
may we know
the love you gazed upon
at Calvary.

(For notes on Simon of Cyrene see pages 10–11.)

## 5. Simon Helps Jesus to Carry His Cross

i.

*Simon of Cyrene*

Chosen,
or merely ill-fated?
And what's the difference?
Is there a line
between the vagaries of chance
and providence?
A division between accident
and an act of God?
And does the difference lie
not in the event
but in the man?
A terrified man in a garden
has nothing but fear in his nostrils,
though the scent of the rose
has not diminished,
nor its bloom.
God help me,
but God was there
on the streets of Jerusalem.
And I did not perceive him
in that miasma of malice.
There is nothing spiritual
in the stench of a mob.
I tell you,
the air was foul
with the reek of lust,

lust for blood.
And I did not see God in the event.
I saw only the threat
and the danger to myself.

Who expects his whole life to change
by accident?
No one expects, but it happens,
accidents of time and place.
It's a long way from Cyrene
to the Damascus Gate.
Do you know how long?
Well it's not much short
of a thousand miles.
And there's no easy way.
Camels in the wilderness,
mules in the mountains,
not much protection
from thieves and brigands,
even if you pay.
And we couldn't pay
so we obeyed the rules
of the caravan traveller.
Don't trail behind,
stay with the crowd,
and sleep back to back
with your eyes open.

By sea to Joppa
might have been quicker,
if we'd worked our passage,
survived storm, pirates
and rotten timbers.
But I like to feel the earth
beneath my feet.
So I trekked a thousand miles
to arrive at that street corner,

on that day,
at that precise minute.
Now there's accident,
there's chance for you.

With cruel precision,
random elements of circumstance
converge at that moment.
Jesus stumbles.
Mary, aged by his pain
mutely implores the soldier.
The soldier, for a confusion of reasons
decides,
and at that moment,
me, Simon,
the convenient foreigner
arrives.
Random elements, did I say?
Strange isn't it,
how the unpredicted and unrelated
blend,
effortlessly.

Not Roman enough to matter,
not Jewish enough to offend,
not local enough to shame,
a rough kindness in the soldier's choice.
But for me, the fear,
shouldering that beam.
Even the memory of it
shrinks my stomach.
I cursed my luck,
I sweated, I watched.
I wept, and yet,
and yet I would not trade
one drop of that day's sweat.

## ii.

*Simon,*
*compelled,*
*pulled from the crowd*
*and never the same again.*
*Climbing,*
*as if condemned,*
*that accursed hill.*
*Did you protest,*
*resist, struggle?*
*Did you tremble*
*when you touched?*
*Did you feel*
*in that wood*
*the weight*
*that would single you out*
*for all eternity?*

*Lord,*
*pulled towards you*
*I am afraid.*
*I fear change in me.*
*I fear what you see*
*in the world and in myself.*
*I am afraid to follow you.*
*I fear being tied,*
*inextricably,*
*to love that never turns.*
*My instincts*
*are to turn and run.*

*Lord.*
*I am not coerced,*
*or compelled,*
*yet I am drawn,*
*magnetized by sacrifice,*

37

*fascinated by love.*
*I hesitate to touch your cross*
*yet long for courage*
*here and now*
*that I might delight in you*
*always.*

(For notes on Veronica see pages 11–12.)

## 6. Veronica Wipes the Face of Jesus

### i.

*Veronica*

Capernaum,
that's where I saw him first,
but all of Galilee
talked of him, wanted him.
At Peter's house
they gathered at the door,
the whole town, beseeching.
He prayed with them
and blessed and healed.
Nothing was beyond him.
Lepers, the blind,
withered limbs,
withered people,
he made them whole.
People, so sure, so convinced,
you could not get near.
They even lowered a man
through the roof.

There was no show,
no play-acting.
In Peter's house, they say,
his mother-in-law lay sick, with fever.
He took her hand.
Nothing more.
In twelve years,

I saw healers,
muttering incantations,
writhing, shouting,
but all my money bought
was their performance.
And physicians,
travelled, trained,
heavy with wisdom,
whose "ministrations"
left me in worse plight than before.
Nurses, witches, magicians, priests,
I tried,
I tried everything but the final cure,
and I considered that, more times than I can tell.

I cannot tell you
when I knew,
knew that he had merely to think
and my agony would end.
I cannot tell you
when I knew that his being,
his presence, would heal.
But I knew before I saw him.
Even on the fringe of that jostle
I felt intoxicated,
stronger, simply knowing he was there.
A precise feeling, alert,
neat, fresh, sharp.
Touching, actually touching,
and waves, white and wind-lashed
broke *through* me,
through a permeable, transparent body,
a washing, purifying, effervescence,
undulating through and through.
And I was, oh, so, so clean.
He looked at me and said,
"Who touched my robe?"

and they laughed.
Looking at me still, he breathed,
a long, sighing breath,
as if he had been drained of his spirit.
He was as no other man.
I fell to my knees,
as I would before God.
"Daughter," he said,
"your faith has made you whole;
go in peace, and be healed."
And he turned and went,
just like that.

And those same eyes looked at me
through blood and dirt and sweat.
And I, who thought I knew pain
and uncleanliness,
had nothing with which to console,
except the cloth from my head
and tears.
But he knew
as he knew in Galilee
when he looked at me and said,
"Who touched my robe?"

ii.

*Bareheaded*
*Veronica stands before Jesus.*
*Arms outstretched.*
*The greeting of a woman transformed*
*in body and spirit.*

*She does not need to ask,*
*"Are you the King of the Jews?*
*Are you the Messiah?"*
*She knows who he is.*

*From Galilee to Jerusalem*
*she has followed him.*
*Now, pained and distressed,*
*still she follows.*
*Through the hostile crowd,*
*through the soldiers,*
*until she stands before her Lord.*
*The cloth is in her hands,*
*and no one speaks*
*as she comforts him.*

*How gentle the hands*
*that held this cloth*
*against that tormented face.*
*The face that sees*
*not only Hell on earth*
*but the darkness that descends*
*into eternity.*
*Sin has fought, and sensing defeat*
*battles more ferociously.*
*Evil has failed to penetrate*
*his goodness;*
*and in a last frenzy of frustration,*
*hurls itself in fury*
*against his body.*
*In this face*
*is the agony of God;*
*God who is love;*
*who took flesh and dwelt amongst us.*

*Lord,*
*whose love healed Veronica,*
*healed the crippled and blind,*
*and defeated sin,*
*heal us, with that same love*
*that we may resist*
*everything that cripples goodness.*

THE STATIONS OF THE CROSS

This station on the Via Dolorosa is in the midst of the
shops and stalls. Jesus would have had to negotiate corners
and steps on a continuing upward incline, an easy place to
stumble beneath the weight of a great burden.


## 7. Jesus Falls for the Second Time

### i.

*Soldier*

Tough, callous,
hard-bitten, thick-skinned,
that's the soldier's set,
the soldier's look.
That's what his buckles and straps,
his uniform, is for,
to give the soldier's look.
But it don't take much looking
to see beneath his helmet.
Oh, he's a lad all right.
He'll take what's going,
he gives as he gets
and he'll curl your ears
with obscenities.
But he's not a complicated man.
As a rule, he's straight.
You might call him hard,
but I'd rather have a soldier
weeping for his mate
than a merchant in mourning
for his money.

Everybody's dirty work,
that's what we are for.

Which means
that we are at the raw end,
the flesh and blood end,
the weeping and dying end.
We can't wash our hands of things,
like some.
Now that's hardness,
turning your back,
nothing to do with me,
couldn't care less,
don't want to know,
apathy, that's real hardness.
I've seen it,
right across the so-called civilized world.
Cities burn, thousands die
of hunger,
ill-treatment, injustice,
and in the market place
they complain about the prices!

I'm not talking about rulers
or even merchant princes,
but housewives and shopkeepers
with their fingers in their ears.
Now that's hardness, that's callous.
Like the day we crucified the carpenter.
Up those steps we went,
towards David's Tower,
through the shops and stalls,
tables covered in pots
and leather-work;
trinkets, beads, necklaces,
silversmiths, goldsmiths and harness-makers;
sacks of corn, vegetables and fruit.
And he fell, on the steps,
in the middle of the market.

A young man
with a few hours left to live.
It wasn't that people shrank
into the shadows,
they did that,
because he was a mess.
But there was only a pause
in the haggling,
a few furtive glances,
a few noses wrinkled in distaste.
It was just another criminal,
just another death.
Nothing to do with them,
not their concern.
Now that is hardness.
Not like soldiers, no
'cos believe me,
there's a world of difference
between hard of face,
and hard of heart.

ii.

*He who has no sin*
*has looked into the face of sin*
*and felt the blast of its violence,*
*the ugly explosion of self-centredness.*
*Before his eyes*
*all the vile and petty sins,*
*meanness, spite, gossip and greed*
*writhe like worms*
*in the dung of Satanic beasts.*

*On his back*
*the weight of the world's distress*
*presses and presses;*

*every disease,*
*every pain ever felt,*
*every callous act*
*in the history of mankind*
*adds its awful weight*
*until, once again,*
*Jesus falls.*

*Dear God,*
*forgive us that we do so little*
*to lighten the load*
*of the world's suffering,*
*make clean the soil of our minds*
*that your love may take root,*
*and so strengthen us*
*that we might not only stand firm*
*in the face of suffering*
*but attack its cause*
*from within, in your name.*

There is insight into the nature of Christ's life and teaching in the number of women who followed him to the cross. There were groups of devout women who felt it a duty to mourn a condemned man. There were also named women: Mary his mother, Mary Cleopas, Mary Magdala, Salome and the mother of James and Joseph, and "many other women" from Galilee and elsewhere.

His appeal lay in the fact that he treated women on equal terms and restored self-respect even to outcast women such as Mary Magdala and the woman found in adultery. His empathy with women and his unreserved behaviour in public would have been regarded by many with suspicion. Even his own disciples are recorded as being surprised to find him talking to the woman at the well, not because she is a Samaritan, but because she is a woman. Even today there are ultra-orthodox Jews who would find his conduct intolerable.

## 8. Jesus Speaks to the Women of Jerusalem

i.

### A Woman

Don't ask my name.
If you tell my story
just say a woman,
a woman of Jerusalem.
Perhaps you think it macabre
to mourn a man, before his death.
But the mourning of mothers
is not the same as men's.
And what could women do

in the face of such brutality
but mourn,
grieve the loss of gentleness,
and love and healing.
"Weep for yourselves", he said,
"and for your children",
and we did.
For qualities
that men profess to love in women
had been condemned in him.
You cannot argue with people who condemn,
and of course, he didn't.
Pilate asked,
"What harm is there in the man?"
What harm in him indeed
who saved me and many
from harm and more.
It was harmlessness we mourned,
the prosecution of innocence,
goodness condemned.

Guilty, condemned,
but for him, I would lie
beneath the stones of virtuous men.
But their secret is secure,
my story is not shared among such men
for shame.
They meant to use my life
as a means to disgrace him.
They dragged me as a thing,
a thing of no importance,
spitting, not at me, but at his name,
these righteous scribes and pharisees,
using my body as a weapon
to strike at him.
In bareheaded humiliation, struggling
for some last semblance of dignity,

I was thrown at his feet.
"A verdict," they said, "your verdict."
And they knew, and he knew,
that the Mosaic law demanded death
by stoning
for an adulteress.

He did not look at me,
but strangely, bent down,
and with such slowness,
wrote on the ground
with his finger.
I thought he would never answer.
Then, he said,
"Let him who is without sin
cast the first stone."
And again
he wrote on the ground
with his finger.

I waited
for a lifetime of stones
falling one by one,
and then, we were alone.
"Woman, where are they?
Who condemns you?"
I could hardly speak,
"No one, Lord."
"Neither do I condemn you.
Go and sin no more."

He saved me,
my life and more
and I mourn him.
The women of Jerusalem mourn him.
Women, women mourn him.

## ii.

*Woman of Jerusalem,*
*did you know the depth,*
*the vortex of your grief?*
*Did your eyes see,*
*reflected in his,*
*generations of hunger,*
*battles, wars,*
*jungle prisons,*
*gas-chambers,*
*Hiroshima?*
*"Weep for your children.*
*If they will do this*
*in the green-wood,*
*what will they do in the dry?"*

*Father,*
*you have entrusted us*
*with innocence,*
*and with choice,*
*and taught us*
*that the gates of Heaven*
*open wide to childlike trust.*
*But we fail our trust,*
*we do not grow up, but down.*
*Enlighten us in the shadow of Christ,*
*that reaching towards his stature*
*we might truly become*
*Children of God.*

By now Jesus is near the end of his terrible walk and, no doubt, near the end of his physical strength and endurance, so that even with the assistance of Simon of Cyrene he falls again.

## 9. Jesus Falls for the Third Time

### i.

*Mary and Martha*

Mary     Earlier,
days perhaps,
or maybe hours,
in Bethany
we had sat with him
and listened;
and the house had filled
with his fragrance.
But they muttered, the men,
about extravagance,
as if they did not know
the meaning of the word "Messiah".
In that house,
breaking bread with Lazarus,
they talked of money.

Martha    We knew the meaning
of that anointing,
we who had buried Lazarus
and wrestle now
with the fact of his touch
and the sound of his voice.

51

Costly nard and broken alabaster?
Three hundred denarii?
What blasphemous prattle.
Three hundred thousand
would not lift the latch of Heaven's gate
nor purchase one minute,
one breath,
of resurrected life.


*Mary*    Four days dead,
anointed, swathed and sealed;
four days' grief
remembered, mourned, missed
by none more than me
who closed his eyes,
or Martha, whose tears did not stay
the passing of Lazarus.


*Martha*  And I saw him, Jesus,
standing, halfway up the hill,
breathless from the moil of the climb.
And I ran,
full of misery and reproach,
"If only you had been here!"
I thought he offered distant comfort,
saying, "Your brother will rise again",
and my tongue, never slow, replied,
"I know. I know he will rise
in resurrection at the last day,
but if you had been here . . ."
"I am the resurrection and the life",
he said, stilling speech and thought
and time itself.
"Do you believe this?"
And I acknowledged him,

and knew, without question or understanding
that I had known,
long, long before the day
he summoned Lazarus from his tomb.

*Mary*    Outside the city,
on that other hill,
on that desolate mound
with its summit now in sight,
he fell again.
And the sullen sky
darkened the eye of God
like a light extinguished.
Confused by his agony,
tormented by his pain,
bewildered;
we could not understand,
who would summon *him*,
the anointed,
from *his* grave.

ii.

*The devil in us*
*mistakes gentleness for weakness,*
*sneers at humility*
*ignorant of its strength,*
*blind to the courage*
*that lies in meekness.*
*And the Devil smiles*
*when love shrinks from the lover*
*plighted to wealth and status;*
*claps his hands*
*when simplicity trips and slips*
*on the trappings of the proud.*

53

AN IMPOSSIBLE GOD

*For the pride that caused Adam's fall,*
*the serpent conceit,*
*the apple of envy*
*plays tricks beneath the feet of Christ.*
*And the Devil roars his mirthless laugh,*
*when Jesus stumbles and falls*
*for a third time.*

*Dear Lord, forgive us*
*that we have loved material things*
*above spiritual;*
*that we have sought status and reward*
*before service to you;*
*that we have been devoted to trivia,*
*cluttering our lives*
*with things of no eternal value.*
*Teach us to see true reality,*
*the things that survive,*
*the things of lasting worth,*
*the things of the spirit.*

Centurions are sometimes imagined as members of an élite officer class within the Roman army. This was not the case. Centurions were extremely successful soldiers who had worked their way up from the ranks. Achieving a centurion's staff meant in most cases that they had reached the top of the military tree that was open to them. They were hard, professional and senior soldiers with great experience and real authority.

It was the custom at executions, when a condemned man was stripped, for the garments to become the prize of the executioners. The custom is referred to in the gospels and the fact that because Christ's garment had no seam, and therefore could not be divided, the men diced for ownership of it.

## 10. Jesus is Stripped of His Garments

### i.

### The Centurion

There is no fitting word
to describe a crucifixion,
or if there is,
it was conceived in Hell,
where, I trust,
God rots the soul
of the fiend who devised it.
Were I to paint a picture
of a crucifixion,
with executioners,
and ghoulish spectators,
it would be filled with devils,
diabolical spirits,

malevolent sprites,
cloven-hooved demons
who must surely dance
in an ecstasy of evil,
with Beelzebub presiding,
or Lucifer, or Satan,
or whatever name you choose
for the Prince of Darkness.
I'd rather fight a horde
of hairy Barbarians
than witness one crucifixion
in the so-called "line of duty".
By the Gods!
It's a disgusting way
to kill a man.

Twelve years' Imperial Service
and the proud possessor
of a centurion's staff
and the oak-leaf crown
for gallantry in battle.
You don't need much gallantry
to supervise a gibbet
but by God you need oak-leaf courage
to die on one with dignity.
I've seen them weep,
struggle, scream and cry for mercy;
and stoics, in teeth-clenched silence
right to the end. I've saluted them.
I have to be there, so I am there.
But the Galilean,
he was another question altogether.
The death of a criminal I understand,
and I lose no sleep over traitors,
but political guile,
assassination by dupery,
murder by manipulation,

that wrinkles the nostrils.
I could smell the stink
of their pious fraudulence.
Even though they stood
on the outer fringe.
I could see the grim satisfaction,
the covert looks and nods.
Through all the religious garb,
the priestly manners,
I could see their devious minds.
Treachery wafted from them
like the breeze from a stagnant pool.

I offered him the customary drink,
something to stupefy the pain,
though I know of no potion
to blur the viciousness of crucifixion.
They usually drain the cup.
The Galilean took it,
let it touch his lips
and then returned it.
Like a guest going through the motions
of courtesy.
He did it with such grace,
and looked at me so steadily,
I hesitated to proceed.
I could see the executioners
with their eyes on his robe,
like hungry dogs waiting for food.
He closed his eyes, quite briefly,
as if giving consent for me to continue.
I echoed that consent
and in seconds he stood naked
while the men, like scavengers,
searched for a seam to divide the cloth.
There was no seam,
so they diced for it.

And while they gambled
like gross, distorted urchins,
we looked, not on his nakedness
but into his face.

ii.

*How vulnerable love is,*
*how easy to attack.*
*Yet somehow*
*the stripping of Christ*
*does not humiliate,*
*does not reduce him,*
*rather, it increases our awareness*
*of God's love*
*for human frailty.*

*In totalitarian regimes,*
*whenever men attempt*
*to reduce Christ,*
*forbid him,*
*with imprisonments and executions,*
*their efforts fail.*
*In trying to suppress*
*they only intensify his presence.*
*Somehow,*
*the stripped body of Christ*
*magnifies*
*the infinite love of God.*

*Lord, increase our awareness of need.*
*Help us to respond*
*to the cries of the poor and oppressed*
*that we may not be ashamed*
*when we hear you ask,*
*"When I was naked, did you clothe me?"*

58

The barbaric cruelty of this form of execution can only be described as evil. In the idea of the body of Christ being pierced by evil, by all the sins against love that were ever committed, is a profound theme for Lenten prayer and contemplation.

## 11. Jesus is Nailed to the Cross

### i.

*John*

Was it timorous cloud,
fleeing in terror,
that opened the sky
to a shaft of light,
or was it the breath of God?
Was it the sun,
bejewelling blood,
transmuting sweat
to golden dew,
reflecting diamond light
in thorns glistening on his Crown,
or was it glory
that crowned his head?
As on that other mount
beneath another cloud
his face had shone
like the sun,
and his garments glistened
intensely white;
transformed, transfigured,
holy.
Divine metamorphosis,
the Father's declaration

of the nature of his son.
Under a cloud
the Baptist,
wild and alone,
with the promise of God alive in him,
dreamed his restless dreams
and prophesied;
until,
a bird, resting on a rising draught,
drew his eyes
to the light resting
on the Son of Man,
and filled his mind
with knowledge of God.
And I saw,
and followed the Son of Man.

And he on whom the light shone
gave light,
the light of love
in dark and loveless places.
Love revealed him,
and he revealed love,
forgiving, restoring, healing,
reckless in generosity,
life-giving;
turning upside down
man-made virtues and values;
parading a kingdom
whose only purpose is love,
whose only power is love;
passionate only for peace and justice,
he dazzled us with love.

There was mystery in his birth
mystery in his being.
A mystery so great

that when declared
they disputed and denied it,
and turned away.
Under this cloud
his disputed title
fluttered at his head,
completing Pilate's
unconscious hymn of praise,
his litany to the Lord
received by angels
who filled the universe
with haunting "Hallelujahs".

"Jesus of Nazareth
King of the Jews."
        Hallelujah!
"Behold the man."
        Hallelujah!
"I find no harm in him."
        Hallelujah!
"What evil has he done?"
        Hallelujah!
"This just man."
        Hallelujah!
"Jesus, called Christ."
        Hallelujah!
"Behold your King."
        Hallelujah!
"Jesus of Nazareth
King of the Jews."
        Hallelujah!

But the visionary choir
was silenced, pained,
by the discord of a nail.

## ii.

Who can bear to gaze
on such cruelty,
the opposite of love,
the antithesis of the hope of man?
Given a new creation,
a second heaven,
rich in mountains, lakes,
fields and trees,
given dominion
over every living creature,
given sunshine and laughter,
given ability to remember,
and to love;
like spoiled brats
stamping our feet
we have taken the gifts
and dashed them to the ground.
We have desecrated the earth,
polluted the seas,
wrought savagery
on our fellow men
and spat in the face of God.
Each bitter deed,
each unlovely act,
each vile thought
pierces Christ,
crucifies love.
Yet from that cross
he prayed,
"Father, forgive them,
they know not what they do."
Such love is measureless,
beyond all deserving.

## THE STATIONS OF THE CROSS

*Lord.*
*As I look at you*
*on the cross,*
*help me to die*
*to that obsession with self*
*that diminishes faith,*
*reduces hope,*
*wearies love,*
*and ultimately, consumes me.*
*Resurrect me,*
*to life in those I have been given to love.*
*Let love redeem me.*

The significance of the death of Jesus is heightened by
the intensity with which these last hours and minutes are
described in the gospels. The years of Jesus's ministry are
described with scant attention to time and dates, but the
last hours of Jesus's life are described in very great detail
from hour to hour, even from minute to minute, right up
to his final breath.

## 12. Jesus Dies on the Cross

### i.

#### Mary, the mother of Jesus

There was always mystery in the child,
yet not surprise, fear perhaps,
yet even my fears seemed inevitable.
Pain and joy, beyond belief, seemed inseparable,
and throughout, the awareness of mystery.
And now,
the mystery of his dying
reached out and touched
the mystery of his birth.
How can I tell you?
Words that embrace mystery do not exist.
Watching, I saw the years weather the child,
mellow the boy, mature the man,
but to see him growing in death
was pain too exquisite even for a mother.
His dying enlarged his life.
The very depth of his agony revealed God
in all the years of his life,
like a veil removed from his soul.
The plunge, that my love could not prevent,

down into the darkness
of that screech-filled pit,
sealed his love in me
and on those who wounded him;
made plain Simeon's prophecy;
revealed the awesomeness,
the otherness of the promise
planted within me,
within the girl betrothed to Joseph.
And as he cried, "Father, forgive them"
I wept, for the mystery of love.

So like him,
the same dying as living.
Healing, reconciling
with forgiveness;
Paralytics, women of the street,
his enemies on every side.
"Go, your sins are forgiven you."
That authority,
that strange authority.
No sad consolation
for the wretched man dying with him,
but emphatic command,
"Amen, I say to you,
this day, you shall be with me
in Paradise."
That poor abused body,
so frail in its suffering,
housing such majesty.

We stood, three Marys,
and John, with his arm about me.
And Jesus looked at us,
and spoke with the same authority.
No pleading, no regrets.
A dying monarch

speaking from his terrible throne,
a son, a loving son
binding those he loved.
"Mother, behold your son."
And to John,
"Behold your mother."
After so long, and so much,
such brevity
– my son.

He left us then
to journey in secret.
He closed his eyes,
and the sky darkened.
The words of the prophet
echoing in my mind.
"Behold, the day of the Lord shall come,
a cruel day.
The sun shall be darkened in his rising
and the moon shall not shine with her light,
and I will visit the evils of the world."
Is that where he was?
Roaming through ages of suffering?
In agony far worse than pain?
Was he being scourged by the evil of years,
nailed with the hatred of centuries?
Had he slid into woeful Hades,
drinking the dregs of men's miseries?
Was his soul being tormented
in the black, despairing caverns
of Hell itself?
Only from depths as deep
could such a cry have rent the air,
and torn at my heart so fiercely
I thought it would destroy me.
"My God! My God!
Why hast thou forsaken me?"

And then he was still,
drained, exhausted.
When he spoke, it was hardly speech,
hardly a whisper:
"I thirst."
The soldiers have a drink,
so bitter it might be vinegar.
One of them offered this,
on a sponge,
and he took it.
He never refused a kindness,
no matter how poor.

Time meant nothing to me then,
I only knew
that the light was mean and miserable.
I seemed to be sinking into a stupor of grief,
until, with such a strong voice, he cried out,
"It is finished!"
and I prayed a prayer of thanksgiving,
but still he spoke,
"Father, into your hands
I commend my spirit."

In the silence I breathed my "Amen",
and then the thunder
shook the earth.

ii.

*Strangely,*
*in the sorrow of this moment,*
*there is hope.*
*In the cry "It is finished!"*
*there is relief.*
*The relief of every soul*

67

*who reaches the end of suffering,*
*the end of pain,*
*the end of anxiety and fear.*
*The end of struggle.*
*Grief is eased by this knowledge.*
*The anguish of life*
*is finally cushioned by death.*
*Dying may be cruel and hard,*
*but death is merciful.*

*Jesus,*
*through your cross,*
*we know that death*
*does not take us into unexplored darkness.*
*The path has been trodden by your feet.*
*In you, crucified Lord,*
*earthly disaster*
*has become hope eternal.*

Normally a hardened professional soldier who had super-
vised many executions would have shut himself off, would
have been emotionally detached, from the execution of a
criminal. For such a man to be drawn into the event, and
to comment that the executed man was both good and the
Son of God, suggests that this execution was out of the
ordinary.

# 13. Jesus is Taken Down from the Cross

## i.

### The Centurion

Never a death like this,
and I've lost count.
Nor will I see its like again.
Dying men cling to life, you know,
even hanging on a cross.
Strong men can last for days.
For what? you might well ask.
Give up, get it over with,
that would make more sense.
But no, they usually struggle.
To see just one more dawn?
Hear a bird?
Feel the breeze,
hear a voice, just once more?
Or perhaps they hope beyond hope
for reprieve, to be taken down.
I don't know.
But they don't go easily.
They don't choose to go.
But he did.

His struggle wasn't with death.
Death was his servant,
not his master.
That wasn't a defeated man.
He was in command to the end.
And then, he gave up his spirit.
It wasn't taken from him,
he gave it up.
He fought a battle from the cross,
but not with death.

I never got to the bottom
of whatever trumped-up charges
put him on that gibbet,
but there wasn't a ghost of guilt about him.
Some said he was a prophet,
but he was more than that,
much more.
On the cross,
his conflict was with something far greater
than bitter-tongued pharisees;
he ignored them,
as dross scattered in the wind.
No, he fought a different battle
and I caught something of it.
I could sense it.
I could almost smell it.
And when he cried out,
something in Hebrew I think,
as if he had been wounded,
I gripped my sword.
I would have fought
if I could have seen the enemy.
But he pulled through.
Later, he gave a great cry of victory.
They were puzzled,
but I know battles and fighters.

I'd recognize a victor's shout,
anywhere.

You do not expect nobility
in the squalor of a crucifixion,
it is meant to humiliate.
You do not expect magnanimity
in the face of cruelty,
pain usually erases that.
Solemnity splattered by obscenity.
Silence in a welter of abuse.
Dignity surviving malicious wounds.
You do not expect majesty
to bleed from a cross,
nor a king to be enthroned
on a scaffold,
but that is what these eyes witnessed,
the transformation of a bestial ceremony
into a coronation.
If innocence could be seen
it was in his eyes.
If truth could be heard
it was in his voice.
If regality exists
it has his face.
If God exists
then this was his son.

Like courtiers,
they lifted down his body,
the cloak of sovereignty
entrusted to their care;
the ornate robe of the conqueror,
his sceptre and orb
temporarily laid aside.

ii.

*Lord,*
*from the cross*
*did you descend into Hell?*
*Did that awful cry*
*burst into history*
*having journeyed from unfathomable depths,*
*from that black hole,*
*millenniums deep,*
*dug by the claws*
*of every sin against love*
*since the beginning of time?*
*Did you descend where faith dies,*
*hope shrivels,*
*where love is incarcerated,*
*forbidden and forgotten?*
*Did you battle on our behalf,*
*resurrecting faith,*
*restoring hope,*
*releasing love to conquer*
*and ascend*
*beyond the reach of all evil,*
*for all time?*

*Lord,*
*we cannot measure your sacrifice.*
*Our minds cannot encompass*
*the extent of your suffering,*
*nor sound the depths*
*of your love.*
*We can only confess*
*that you are the son*
*of the God of love.*

The tomb is provided by a rich man, one bold enough to face the Roman governor and ask for the body of Jesus. The description of the tomb is very exact: it is owned by Joseph of Arimathea, very recently dug out of solid rock and sealed with a large stone.

## 14. Jesus is Placed in the Tomb

### i.

*Joseph of Arimathea*

Nicodemus had been bolder,
spoken to him, questioned him,
spent sleepless nights
wrestling with his answers.
Of course we awaited the Messiah,
for hundreds of years we waited,
and looked at this warrior,
at this leader, at this prophet.
We had sat at the feet of great rabbis,
been disturbed by the Baptist,
shaken by the Nazarene,
his preaching and his acts.
Of course we asked,
"Is this he?"
But the gnat that startled the ear,
irritated the eye;
the thorn, the itch beneath the skin
that became unbearable,
was the fact that he was not subject
to our law,
the law was subject to him.
He was followed by ruffians and harlots,

so we doubted.
Such paradox,
such extravagance,
a multi-coloured larva,
a caterpillar of brilliant hue
amongst decaying leaves,
beautiful but defiled.
An exciting brilliance and vulnerable
to eye and claw;
exquisite and doomed.

Nicodemus talked with me.
We argued, disagreed, speculated
and watched his progress.
He spoke not of a future paradise
but a present Kingdom;
of judgement passed upon ourselves.
"God so loved the world
that he gave his only Son,
that whoever believes in him
should not perish but have eternal life.
For God sent the Son into the world,
not to condemn the world,
but that the world might be saved
through him.
He who believes in him is not condemned;
he who does not believe is condemned already."
He spoke of God offering life,
not condemnation,
refusal of that life was its own condemnation,
not God's.
He spoke of the Son of Man
descended from Heaven,
and preached with that authority.
And still, we watched from the shadows.
We could not rush after him
waving branches like children.

We are old men, Nicodemus and me.
We heard him speak as a boy.
He astonished us then.
Even then he spoke of being
"about my father's business".
Even then,
he behaved as a son like no other son.

At the cross, we knew.
Like listening to an argument
in which bluster and noise
is substituted for reason,
and the silence of certainty
is louder for its stillness.
Noise may win majorities,
but it does not alter truth.

At the end
it was we two,
the doubters from the shadows,
who faced Pilate,
we prevaricators
who saw him lifted down,
who bought the linen
and provided the tomb.
We old men
wanting to be born anew,
we, who saw that his corpse
was not so much a lifeless body,
as a shell vacated,
a husk, a chrysalis.

ii.

*They could not see,*
*nor understand*

75

*as they laid his body in the tomb,*
*that death had been defeated.*
*They could not comprehend*
*that the Son of Man*
*could not be sealed with a stone.*

*Buried beneath a mountain*
*and guarded with armies,*
*his life would have burst it asunder*
*and scattered legions.*
*But that is not the way*
*of the Son of God.*
*In silence, he turned the world upside down,*
*and left the tomb,*
*not shattered, but tidy,*
*like a thoughtful guest,*
*leaving early.*

*Lord, forgive us,*
*the doubters in the shadows.*
*Forgive us our prevarications,*
*our cynical speculation.*
*When you offer eternal life*
*let us not condemn ourselves*
*in the pride of shallow wisdom.*
*Lord, we believe,*
*help our unbelief.*

# III.   The Stations
Beyond the Cross

# The Stations Beyond the Cross

The first doubters and disbelievers of the resurrection of Jesus Christ were not the enemies of Jesus but his friends. Mary Magdala's announcement to the apostles that she has seen the risen Jesus is not believed. The apostles were realistic, pragmatic artisans. They had no illusions about death, so they dismissed Mary's witness as the effects of grief, but in the end the "impossible" had to be accepted even by them.

## 1. Jesus Appears to Mary Magdalene

### i.

*Mary Magdalene*

Oh, I know you,
and I have known you,
you priests and lawyers;
your lessons in forgiveness,
your talk of penance,
your wise reckoning
of the requirements of restitution,
your pious reflections
on ritual cleansing.
Sages, with such gravity,
rearranging lives
like weary flowers.
Would you rearrange

the crushed stem of my life?
Would you counsel me,
give comfort in the light of day
as I did in the shadows?

Oh, I know you,
my dear, sweet doctors of the law,
as you did not know me
when the sun had risen.
"Mary, be reasonable.
Your name's a byword,
you are, ritually, untouchable,
unclean, contemptible,
a prostitute,
a thing on which to spit,
in daylight.
Sin favours the freedom of darkness;
with the coming of the sun
another face, another voice is required.
You do understand, Mary, don't you?"

Did your heart flutter,
were you uneasy,
did you wonder what he knew
when he said,
"Let him who is without sin
cast the first stone"?
Did you remember me
when he called you hypocrites?
Did you feel that he could see
into the dark corners of your mind,
when he measured you with those words,
"White-washed sepulchres,
clean on the outside
and rotten within"?
Such a man must have terrified you,
a man who could see into your soul;

as he terrified me,
with his love.

I was afraid of him
and afraid for him
from the day we met.
How can a man be gentle
and reckless at the same time?
It was as if that poor body
could hardly contain the love within him.
He embraced my past,
all the pain,
all the mistakes;
enveloped them,
made me feel like a child,
a laughing child.
So much love
I ached with joy.

But the fine men,
councillors and lawyers,
saw only yesterday's sins
and censured him;
reviled his generosity
and laid our sins at his feet.
They could not see, they would not see.

To such blindness
the Devil is a willing guide.
His demons led them
deep into conspiracy,
used their fears as stepping stones;
with devious cunning
put them on the path of twisted truth;
beguiled them with indignation
'til they became at one

with the purpose of the Prince of Darkness;
committed to blotting out
the love that offers life.
Without that light
we plunged into gloom
beyond our comprehension.
The Temple veil was ripped, they say,
torn apart to reveal
the emptiness of their secret place,
the barrenness of that tabernacle.
The Holy of Holies
had been sealed with a stone.
And that closed sepulchre
entombed my heart, reduced my life
to a sleep of grief.

Hardly awake,
I saw a single drop of dew, a jewel
studded in a gnarled and ancient tree,
an amethyst trapping the sun,
capturing colours I could change
by the slightest movement of my head,
from sparkling purple to sapphire,
to brilliant white, to burnished gold.
A breath shimmered the leaves
and cobwebs strung with crystals
glittered in the olive green
as though a hand had scattered diamonds
in its branches.
A morning sun, so clear, so bright,
my eyes averted,
lowered in natural obeisance to its power.
Yet in its warmth was comfort.
What instinct, what feeling,
what presentiment informed me
that this rising of the sun was singular?
With slow majesty

that colossus of fire lifted
and displayed a vast,
mountain-dwarfing sky.
No cloud, no wisp, no sound.
In such silence
I should have heard
the still, small voice
calling to his son.

On the hill
only the song of birds
breached the silence.
In those few minutes
before we reached the tomb
the earth held its breath.
We looked at each other,
aware of the intensity,
napes prickling.
Something was about to happen,
or had happened.
Even the natural orders,
sun, sky and hills,
seemed awestruck, stunned.
Golgotha had changed.
Grief had drained into gullies
and all the pain of that dread day
had been washed into the valley.
The stones cleansed
with light.

And there was the tomb,
open, and empty.
Who can count ripples
seething over stones
in a rapid stream,
or recall the tracery
of dappled light

beneath a summer tree?
The hours of that day
were no less brilliant,
no less confused.
The sounds of a moment,
brief images, glimpses,
surface in a sea of memories.
Peter, outside the tomb,
afraid and inconsolable,
drained, hollow-eyed,
wiping sweat from his brow,
from his hands.
John, tight-lipped, resolute,
a lost boy
determined not to weep.
But, oh, how long
is a minute of eternity?
How can I measure
the incandescent splendour
that radiated from his face,
or recapture the joy,
the tremble of exquisite,
unspeakable bliss
at the sound of his voice?
"Mary, do not hold me.
I have not yet ascended
to the Father."
But I had touched him,
and touching and hearing and seeing
I knew the sanctity, the holiness,
the invincibility of his love.
In the upper room,
I remember the anger
that surged through me
in the face of disbelief.
How else could I convince them?
What else could I say?

"I have seen the Lord", I said.
"He spoke to me."

I left them
and sat outside
on the steps, in the sun,
until my anger dissolved
into tears, and my body shook
with silent laughter
at the joy which would be theirs.

ii.

*Would that I were half as true*
*as Mary of Magdala;*
*possessed of a quarter*
*of her loyalty;*
*enriched by an eighth*
*of her love.*

*In the face of taunts*
*I am silent.*
*With pretended ignorance*
*I deny.*
*With sycophantic smiles*
*I persecute.*

*Risen Lord,*
*forgive me.*
*In your mercy, catch me*
*with the love*
*that captured Mary Magdalene,*
*that I may, with courage,*
*look upon your suffering*
*in all its manifestations;*
*know your will*

*in every act of love;*
*share your joy*
*in innocence and repentance;*
*grow in your faith,*
*and in truth declare,*
*"I have seen the Lord."*

The story of the resurrection of Christ from the dead does not ask us to cast aside our doubts but rather our convictions, which is exactly what the people at Emmaus had to do. They had to throw away their convictions about what happens to people after they have died.

## 2. Jesus Appears at Emmaus

### i.

*Cleopas*

A stranger,
full of energy and life,
striding from behind
overtook us, and asked,
"What's the news?"

Dear God! Was he a Jew
leaving Jerusalem this day
and did not know the news?
But he knew
more than we had ever known.
Yet still, our death-filled eyes
failed to see him.

We are flesh and blood.
We know what we can feel and see and touch,
and in Jerusalem
we had seen a dead man,
beaten, nailed, pierced,
the breath driven from his body.
That was what they took down from the cross,
that was what they sealed in the tomb,

a lifeless thing, a corpse,
a dead man.
Bereaved,
how deep the shadows
of dusk,
how void the mind,
how hollow the groans
from sorrow's cross,
how dimmed the eye
to all but grief and loss.

With leaden feet,
we two had made our descent
from Jerusalem's rocky peak,
along the Emmaus track,
our backs towards the stone-sealed tomb.
In snatches, and half-completed phrases
we had remembered,
conversations, laughter, and bread
shared beside the dusty way.
Hopelessly, we remembered
that we had seen the eyes,
touched the hands
and heard the voice that had promised life,
had given life.

By the sea,
and in the hills,
listening, we had thrilled
to visions of hope beyond all dreaming.
And now we were without hope, empty,
for he was dead,
indisputably, cruelly, bloodily dead.

And then we ate,
or rather sat at table;
we had no appetite.

He would have gone on,
like some pilgrim
anxious to visit the entire world.
We did not want him to go.
In his company
the miles had slipped away beneath our feet.
Somehow, there was comfort in his presence
that made our misery more bearable.
Somehow, his words stirred within us
the still warm ashes of hope.
"It's late", we said.
"Share our table and stay the night."

Yes, we have asked,
"Why did we not see?"
But have unopened eyes ever seen him?
Vast crowds had heard him preach,
seen him heal the lame, the withered and the blind,
restore madmen to sanity
and even breathe life into the dead.
They had heard words.
They had seen miracles,
but they had not seen him.
And he had known.
"Seeing they do not see,
and hearing they do not hear."

We thought we had seen and heard.
We thought that we were among the chosen.
Together, with him,
we led the march towards the new kingdom,
but the road led to Gethsemane, Golgotha and
    death.
And such a death,
mean, sordid and bestial,
strung up between a couple of common thieves.
Hearing, we had heard what we wanted to hear.
Seeing, we had seen what we had wanted to see.

Even on the Emmaus road
we did not hear him.
As he sat at table
we did not see him
until he broke bread.

Then we saw madness staring us in the face,
wild, incredible insanity!
Our logic, our intelligence,
our understanding of things as they are
was destroyed in a moment of seeing.
For one stomach-shrinking, breath-robbing,
brain-whirling fraction of time
we were unhinged!
What we called "our wits"
staggered to the brink of lunacy,
teetered at the edge,
scrabbled helplessly
at the storm-blasted rags of reason
and then pitched, headlong,
into that delirious, visionary, idiotic joy
that rational minds can never know.
He is alive!
Jesus of Nazareth,
that blood-drained,
crucified,
dead and buried man,
is alive!
Doctors, lawyers, philosophers,
conquering kings, rulers and emperors
have, with their lives,
scratched the surface of history.
Jesus of Nazareth,
in a moment,
has split open every human concept of history.
He is alive!

No ghost –
no ethereal spirit,
ghosts do not cast shadows.
Men cast shadows, and this was a man,
a bread-breaking, food-eating man.

And then our ecstasy turned to fear,
awesome fear.
Had we passed out of time?
We could see the room,
chairs and tables were solid.
Wine, bread, fruit in the bowl
had not changed.
The light declared the lateness of the hour.
The hour!
The world had turned upside down
in a hundredth part of a second!
In that part of that second,
his words came leaping,
like flaming torches into our heads.
"In my Father's house are many mansions . . ."
"This temple will be destroyed
and in three days . . ."
"Where I go you cannot follow."
"I go to prepare a place for you."
We had looked for a Messiah.
We had looked for a new king in Israel,
and sitting at our table
was the Lord of Life and Death,
the Lord of Time,
the King of Eternal Life,
the King of All Creation,
the King of Kings,
Alpha and Omega!
"The Father and I are one."

We could not speak,
we dared not speak the name
of him who broke bread
at our table.
We were the living dead,
brought to life in a moment
by his presence.

And then he was gone.
And being divinely mad
we were not surprised.
The Lord of Everlasting Life
is not enslaved
by time or space.

And now,
although our eyes no longer behold his face,
we see him,
as we have never seen him before.


ii.


*Lord,*
*how often have I walked the Emmaus road*
*in your company,*
*and not seen you.*
*How often has my myopic faith*
*looked on the pilgrim Christ*
*and perceived only a sympathetic traveller.*
*How often have I been deaf*
*to words of love and healing,*
*been within reach of touching*
*the hem of the robe of the risen Christ*
*and in utter self-assurance,*
*unaware of my blindness,*
*ignored the pierced hand*
*stretched out for me.*

## THE STATIONS BEYOND THE CROSS

*Dear Lord,*
*am I entirely to blame*
*that I do not expect*
*at my kitchen table*
*to sit in the presence of eternal love?*
*Such love belongs to another world.*
*The only fit setting for divine love*
*is with Angels and Archangels,*
*Cherubim and Seraphim,*
*heavenly choirs, saints and martyrs triumphant.*
*How can the heavenly banquet*
*be set at my table?*

*Is it surprising*
*that I do not expect the Christ*
*for whom the Temple veil was ripped in two,*
*for whom the earth darkened and thunder roared,*
*to break bread with me?*
*Is it surprising*
*that I do not expect the Christ*
*who conquered death and opened the gates of*
    *Heaven*
*to sit at a table*
*where nothing more is offered*
*than cold chicken, plain bread and home-made*
    *wine,*
*and fruit, past its best?*
*Yet even as I think these things*
*I hear you whisper,*
*"Seeing, they do not see,*
*and hearing they do not hear."*

*Dear Unexpected Lord,*
*a banquet with you*
*is bread shared with friends.*
*You did not sit with rulers and kings*
*but with fishermen, carpenters and shepherds.*

*Your seamless robe was not silk or satin
but the homespun cloth of the village hearth.
You began your earthly days
wrapped in makeshift strips of cloth
surrounded by sheep and oxen
and people in ragged clothes,
a ruler without ornament.*

*But love needs no ornament.
Love is your garment.
Love is your crown.
Love is your kingdom.
Love is your healer.
Love is your restoring forgiveness.
Love is your joy.
Love is the life you offer.
Love is the bread you break.*

*The presence of your love
turns kitchens into palaces,
homes into royal courts,
hearts into temples.
In your presence
every table is a heavenly banquet.*

*Lord,
heal my blindness,
open my eyes to see you
on every country road and city street.
Open my ears to hear you
in every conversation
with family, friend and stranger.*

*Awaken me,
bring me to life
that I might know
that where there is pain*

you weep.
Where famine strikes
and wide-eyed children wail
your voice cries, "I thirst".
When arrogance and violence
strut across my path
may your forgiving word
be in my heart.
When love is persecuted and oppressed
may I see your thorn-crowned head.

When trees shiver
may I feel your nearness.
In the mystery of mountains,
in the power of the sea,
in the wonder of the skies
may I celebrate your endless love.
Lord, in your mercy,
may I never break bread
without giving thanks
for the body broken for me,
and in your risen presence
may every meal
be my Emmaus.

Most pictures of the supper at Emmaus assume that the two disciples were men. I see no good reason for this. One of the two is named as Cleopas. We know that Mary, the wife of Cleopas, was present at the crucifixion of Jesus. So it would seem highly likely that the two followers of Jesus returning to their home in Emmaus were, in fact, man and wife, Mary and Cleopas.

## 3. Jesus Appears to the Disciples

### i.

*Mary, wife of Cleopas*

How brisk,
how light and lively,
how swift
are joyous feet.
How restored by hope
are weary limbs.
Hope,
which quickens the step
and sets the spirit in search
of new melody.
How fresh, how sudden the change
in rhythm and tune
for those who had shared
in Calvary's dirge.
Each mile to Emmaus
was measured in years,
such was the burden,
the drag of sorrow's weight.
But that same steep climb
to David's city

96

could not slow feet
winged with joy.

We entered the gate
at evening.
Shutters drawn on streets abandoned
to the scurry of rodents
and the stalking of cats.
But darkness could not dim
the light of our experience,
nor quench the flame
of his life within us.

We gave the sign
and were admitted.
We could not wait;
before the bar secured the door
we declared,
"We have seen the Lord!"
And immediately
they spoke of Mary Magdala
and Simon Peter,
in confusion and doubt,
until confusion was compounded
by his presence.

In our shocked and fearful silence
he greeted us.
"Shalom", he said,
and lifting his hands
we saw the imprints,
the marks of the crucified.
As ever, he saw within.
"Why are you troubled?" he said,
"touch me and see,
a ghost does not have flesh, as I have."

And whilst we questioned
the testimony of our eyes
he smiled and asked for food.
Fish they gave him,
broiled fish,
and he sat and ate before us.
And once more he began to teach
and they listened
as they had in Galilee.

As he spoke
the wonder of his being enfolded me,
and the wonder of my being in his presence
changed again my conceptions
of reality.
Death, time, space,
spirit, body,
all were one.
All were now his servants.
His eating was for us,
for our inability to understand his nature.
His voice was real,
his wounds were real,
the fish was digested.
Material things for material people.
Flesh and spirit were his to command.
Yet as he spoke,
I looked and saw
the years of his body
in the lines of his face,
and the burden of the cross
in his eyes.

I had to tell myself,
remind myself,
that I had stood at the cross;
watched him die;

seen his body without breath;
recognized the moment
when the light of life
had gone out;
seen the mask of death
compose his face;
seen death certified
with a thrust of a spear.
And now, three days later
at this table,
he sat, talking.

In that moment,
the madness of Emmaus,
the vision of his triumph over death,
his lordship of time and space,
lifted me to a new reality.
I saw that three days,
three years, three hundred years
had no power over him.
In that moment,
in the whirling of my brain,
I could see him
sitting at a thousand tables,
in a thousand places,
even as I gazed upon his face
in that barred and bolted upper room.
In that moment I knew
that the singing in my heart,
the music in my head,
the joy in my body,
the excitement, the fear,
the holy havoc inside me
was his transformation
of love, into worship.

## ii.

Lord,
in millions of rooms
and in this room,
I am in your presence.
Though the doors of my soul
are bolted and barred,
enter in.
Calm my anxieties and fears,
restore my hope,
remove my doubt,
and give me peace.

May I look upon your face
and know the Father's love.
May I see in your eyes
the forgiveness that restores
and heals my failures of faith.
May I hear in your voice
the truth that makes me whole.
May I know in your word
the reality of life in your spirit.

May my love become worship.
May my days give praise.
May my life acknowledge
the glory of the living Son
of the living God,
the Lord of Life.

Doubting Thomas is often considered to be a rational thinker whose doubts are intellectual. I think the scriptural evidence suggests he was simply a plain man who did not understand what was going on. He it was who asked Jesus, "How can we know the way if we don't know where you are going?" I believe this was not a deep existentialist question but simply a pragmatic enquiry. When the other apostles are trying to persuade Jesus to keep out of Jerusalem because they know there are plots to kill him, it is Thomas who says, "If he is going to die, then let us go and die with him." I suspect the others groaned at his unsophisticated approach to the situation they were in.

## 4. Jesus Appears to Thomas

### i.

### *Thomas*

I know what they say,
that I'm impulsive,
bull-headed, loyal
but not very bright.
"Thomas, the twin,
his brother got the brains."
Well, that's as may be,
but faith has nothing to do with brains,
just as belief has little to do with seeing.
And I did believe in him,
enough to want to die with him
even before I knew who he was.

I was with him from the beginning,
and I can tell you,
it was not three years
of palm branches and Hosannas.
He may have had no fear,
or at least he didn't show it,
but those crowds worried us.
It needed only one hot-head
with a stone in his hand.
The loudest voice
is the mind of the mob.
That's why we crossed the Jordan.
When men use the word "blasphemer",
they're looking for a reputation
or an excuse for a stoning.
So we crossed the Jordan
for safety.

It was Lazarus
who brought us to Bethany.
Most of us wanted to stay
where it was safe,
where people honoured the memory
of the Baptist,
remembered and believed
his prophecy about Jesus.
Yes, it was safe
across the Jordan.
But he said, "Lazarus is asleep",
and they argued, "Then he will recover
– we should stay here
– it's too dangerous in Bethany."
"Lazarus is dead", he said.
"Let us go to him."
I knew he had decided,
and I was prepared
to go wherever he went,

and said so to the others,
"If he is going, and you think he'll die
then let's go, and die with him."

I was always committed to him,
stubborn, mule-headed, if you like.
Even at that last supper,
in the upper room,
I wanted to go on, with him.
But he spoke in riddles
about where he was going,
about our "knowing the way".
I like things plain, so I asked
"If we don't know where you are going,
how can we know the way?"
And he said,
"I am the way."
It was not that I didn't trust him
– not that I didn't believe him.
I simply did not understand.

I did not understand him.
I did not understand his trial.
I did not understand Pilate
giving him up to be crucified.
I told you, I'm a plain man,
but I did understand his death.
There's only one type of man
comes down from a cross,
a dead man.
That I do know.

And I wasn't the only one
who didn't believe he'd come back.
Nobody believed Mary Magdala.
"It's an idle tale", they said.
"A woman's grief", they said.

103

And I could understand that.
People do think they've seen
husbands, wives, children,
after their death.
I can understand that.
In grief people think of little else.
The more you've loved
the more you cling to the memory,
afraid of not being able to recall
the eyes, the voice, the face.
And Mary, well,
who could have loved more
than Mary?

Who could I have believed?
They were all in a state.
Within twenty-four hours
Judas had hanged himself
and Jesus was crucified.
Simon Peter was beside himself
with remorse.
Everyone was shattered.
And they're all, well,
a bit more fanciful than me.
Not that I wasn't stricken with grief,
I was. So much so, I couldn't abide
notions that would upset me more,
turn and twist me inside out.
But they kept insisting
'til I could bear it no longer,
until I shouted at them,
"I do not believe you!
Unless I see in his hands
the print of the nails,
and place my finger
in the mark of the nails,
and place my hand in his side,

I will not believe!"
After that, they left me alone.

Then he came.
That familiar face,
that quiet voice,
"Shalom", he said.
"Thomas, put your finger here,
and see my hands,
put out your hand,
and place it in my side,
do not be faithless, believe."

Oh, if I had words
to tell you what I saw,
for I saw everything and nothing
in the bat of an eye,
I saw lepers and blind men,
the sick, the lame, the palsied.
I saw Lazarus, and storm-stilled waters,
saw the crowds, heard him teach,
saw him break bread,
heard him say, "This is my body."
But most of all I saw him;
and at the same time
realized that I knew nothing,
that eternity would not be deep enough
to sound the depths
of the man before me.
In his wounds were chasms of love
with shafts so deep, I knew
that I could never measure
the love that asked me to touch.
A waterfall of revelations
had cascaded over me.
I could not move.
I could only pray,
"My Lord and my God!"

Then he spoke again,
"Thomas,
have you believed
because you have seen me?
Blessed are those
who have not seen
and yet believe."

I could not even claim
to have believed
because of what I'd seen.
I did not deserve faith,
I did not achieve faith.
Faith came as a gift.

I had seen him
for years,
I had heard his words
for years,
I had known his love
for years,
but I had not believed
what my eyes told me.
I had heard a man say,
"He who sees me,
sees him who sent me",
but I was blind
until the Spirit revealed him
as he was and is,
and always shall be,
my Lord and my God.

ii.

*My Lord and my God,*
*who has granted me*

*the gift of faith,*
*hear me when I pray,*
*"Lord, I believe,*
*help my unbelief."*

*Lord, I am easily diverted,*
*side-tracked, confused.*
*So often I balance precariously*
*on the edge of unbelief.*
*Risen Lord,*
*when my prayers seem to echo*
*with hollowness,*
*fill the void.*
*When I am alone,*
*speak to me.*
*When I am in darkness,*
*be my light.*
*When the faith I possess*
*begins to slip my grasp,*
*secure it for me.*
*When I begin to doubt your love,*
*reveal yourself to me*
*as you did with Thomas,*
*that with him I might pray,*
*"My Lord and my God".*

The return to Galilee was perhaps inevitable: most of the Apostles came from Galilee. It was here that they could earn a living, and it was here that they had listened to and learned the gospel of their Lord. It was a place redolent with memories of Jesus.

## 5. Jesus Appears on the Beach at Galilee

i.

*Peter*

A good man, Zebedee,
and a good fisherman too,
the boat told you that;
clean, neat repairs,
timbers as tight as a drum.
She hadn't lain idle.
He'd kept her in use.
It's the only way for a working boat.
They open up and die
out of water.
I examined everything,
lashings, spars, oars,
sails, fishing gear,
oil for the flares.
She was ready.
No, she hadn't been idle
and neither had old Zebedee.

There were seven of us,
a good number, seven.
We'd agreed in Jerusalem

that we'd work together.
We couldn't stand idle,
had to earn a living,
but everyone seemed reluctant
to make a start,
so I took the lead.
Just told them,
"I'm going fishing tonight."
I knew they'd come,
and they did.

A strange night,
with more memories than fish.
A night for dreaming,
too much and too long.
There's mystery at night on Galilee.
Lake Kinnaret we call it,
which means
"the harp-shaped sea".
Kinnaret is not the "harp" of Israel
but the heart.
It is a living thing,
with Jordan as its life-stream,
the life-blood of the land.
Deep down she lies,
silver and night-black liquid
lapping the feet of mountain giants.
But it was a haunted and haunting night.
The ghosts of the past
slipped along the shore
as we eased out of Bethsaida.
It seemed that we were followed
by the cries of our childhood
travelling on the water,
and I imagined I was watched
by the eyes of him
whose sight had been restored

in Bethsaida.
To the west
Capernaum winked,
before the shutters closed her eyes
on the stories locked within her walls,
and her ears
on the echoes of his preaching.
In my mind I saw
the paralysed man being lowered
from the roof.
Heard the Centurion's plea,
"Say but the word,
and my servant shall be healed."

Beyond Capernaum's walls
lay Tabgha,
the place of seven springs,
where one summer's day
five loaves crumbled
to fill a dozen baskets.
And in silhouette against the sky
the mount, and the sermon
moved me once again.

Then Thomas asked,
"When shall we light the flare?"
He at least remembered
our task was luring fish.
Before the flame reduced my sight
I saw in the distance
the shape of Roman villas,
their settlement, Tiberias,
and recalled the crowds
who clamoured through the town
to catch a glimpse,
not of Roman splendour,
but of a carpenter
from Nazareth.

To the east lay Hippos
where the Greeks had built their town
to crown a hill,
before the Romans came.
And to the north of Hippos
the bones of Gadarene swine
lay rotting in the sea.

All night long we fished,
casting and hauling,
but only memories surfaced
to swirl around our heads
until cold, first light
heralded the dawn.

Nathanael said,
"There's someone on the beach."
I looked to the land
and saw a man.
He shouted,
"Have you caught any fish?"
"No", we answered.
"Cast your net
on the right side of the boat,
and you will find some."
Now it's a curious thing,
which you learn if you live
by the waters of Galilee,
that when the sun is low,
as it is at dawn,
from the land
you can see the shadows
of the fins of fish
on the surface,
like leaves on the water.
"He's a local man", I thought.
So we cast the net,
and immediately all seven of us

111

were leaping for the fastenings
as the net plunged deep
and slewed the boat
with the force of it.
"Some" fish!
Did he say, "some"?
The net was alive with them!
The water churned white,
the air loud with the noise of struggle!
Not ten or twenty fish,
or even fifty!
We couldn't count them,
but I knew –
from a life-time on this sea –
that more than a *hundred* fish
strained and tested that net!
Not little fish, but large!
So large and so many
I did not believe the net would hold.
We couldn't haul it in
– dare not!
No fishermen in Galilee
had ever landed such a catch!
"Beach her!" I shouted.
"It's the only way!"
And as they took to the oars
John caught my arm,
"It is the Lord", he said.
I looked.
Of course it was the Lord;
with such a catch,
it had to be!
We were close in.
I grabbed my tunic,
and jumped into the shallows.
The dark night had passed
and this, truly, was the dawn!

On the beach,
the first thing I saw
brought me to a standstill.
It was a charcoal fire.
Like icy water
trickling down the spine,
the joy of seeing him
drained into abject shame.
I would never see a charcoal fire
and not remember my treachery,
my three, fear-crazed denials.
The others gathered round me
and he said,
"Bring me some of the fish
you have just caught."
I turned on my heel
and ran to the boat,
unstoppable tears running down my face.
I tried to overcome them
with energy.
I jumped aboard and freed the net.
Rage at my own guilt
swept through me
as I heaved that massive catch
on to land.
It took time
but I harnessed my fury
until the job was done
and my anger subsided.
It was a miraculous catch.
Without thought, out of habit,
I had counted them.
There were no less
than one hundred and fifty-three fish.
And gathering the net,
I saw it was unbroken,
not one strand had parted.

Jesus said,
"Come and have breakfast."
We sat around him.
He had not needed our catch,
there was fish already on the fire.
Then he took bread
and gave it to us.
He said nothing;
his presence,
the bread,
the action,
said everything.
There was no condemnation,
his fellowship was my reconciliation.
He knew my boasting.
He knew my denials.
He knew the rashness of my promises.
He knew my heart.
He knew my sorrow, my contrition.
Yet he who said,
"I am the bread of life",
said nothing.
His broken flesh offered bread,
and breaking bread with him
we were in communion,
forgiven, healed,
restored to new life.
After breakfast
I walked with him
beside the sea we knew so well
and that familiar boat.
By the boat, he stopped
and with a gesture
that might have included
the sea, the boat
and the men on the beach,
he said,

"Simon, son of John,
do you love me
more than these?"
I said, "Yes, Lord,
you know that I love you."
He said,
"Feed my lambs."
We walked a little further
and he said again,
"Simon, son of John,
do you love me?"
I looked at him,
he neither smiled nor frowned.
Again I replied,
"Yes, Lord, you know that I love you."
He said,
"Tend my sheep."
Then the third time,
as if he doubted me,
he said,
"Simon, son of John,
do you love me?"
I felt that he was examining me
to the root of my soul.
He knew the difference in strength
between my willingness
and my ability.
He knew that I was a leader
who failed.
He knew that I could make foolhardy gestures,
even valiant, or brave,
and then be overcome with fear.
For a third time he asked me.
What more could I say?
Did he simply want
three affirmations of love
to counter my three denials?

Was he saying he expected more?
But I had no more to offer
other than my whole self,
strengths and weaknesses,
courage and fear,
faith and faithlessness.
I said,
"Lord, you know everything,
you know that I love you."
And once again he said,
"Feed my sheep."
And then I saw,
he was not revealing my failures to me,
he was revealing his love,
he was revealing his constancy.
No matter how often I failed him
he would never leave me,
he would always come to me,
recall me to his service.
He did not expect perfection,
only my love, however flawed.
So much made sense
and so much would occupy my thoughts
for the rest of my days.
He was trusting me,
not to be free from sin,
but to keep coming back.
He would do the rest.
"On this rock I will build my Church,
and the gates of Hell shall not prevail."
The Church, like the net,
will not break,
not because of my strength or effort
but because his love
cannot be defeated,
by denials, treachery
or even a cross.

He was not rebuking me,
but offering love,
an impossible constant love.

He told me
that I who led others
would be led one day
to my death.
But I was to follow him.
And he who spoke
stood before me
on the other side of death.
The very thing
I had feared so much,
the root of my fear,
the root of my denials,
death, through my risen Lord,
was not a dark,
invincible power,
but merely a stepping stone
to light, and life eternal.

When I asked him
to tell me John's fate,
he did not laugh out loud,
but there was humour
in his reply.
"Peter, what is that to you?",
and once again
he said,
"Peter, follow me."


ii.


*Risen Lord,*
*I have heard your call*

to follow you
and I have followed
at a distance,
half-heartedly, unsure.
This very day
I hear you call,
"Follow me",
and I will, imperfectly,
easily distracted,
lagging behind when the road is hard.
Lord, forgive me,
reach out to me with your guiding hand
that I might follow you more nearly.

Risen Lord,
I have often seen you
but failed to recognize you.
I become so immersed in my world,
my family, my circle,
that I fail to see you
even when you are on my doorstep.
Wherever there is loneliness,
wherever there is hunger,
wherever there is suffering
you are there.
Wherever there is love,
wherever there is fellowship,
wherever bread is broken in your name
you are there.
Lord, open my heart and mind
that I may see you more clearly.

Risen Lord,
I have heard you ask,
"Do you love me?",
and I reply,
"Yes, Lord, you know that I love you",

*but I have not been loyal,*
*I have not been faithful,*
*I have been full of big promises*
*too easily broken.*
*I have ignored you*
*when love was needed*
*for neighbours or a friend.*
*I live my life*
*as if no one was homeless,*
*no one persecuted,*
*no one in need.*
*Lord, forgive me*
*and teach me gratitude,*
*that seeing the love I have received*
*I might respond with love,*
*and being closer to love,*
*love you more dearly.*

\*

*Most merciful Redeemer, Friend and Brother,*
*may I know you more clearly,*
*love you more dearly,*
*and follow you more nearly*
*day by day.*

*(St Richard)*

The Ascension, like the Transfiguration, is one of those events in which something happened that was outside all previous human experience and for which no adequate words exist to describe what happened. The most complete description is given by Luke in the first chapter of the Acts of the Apostles. However, even with that description, one is left with the impression that whatever happened, the apostles, who are named very precisely, were left in a stunned and awestruck state. They are asked, "Galileans, why are you standing there looking up at the sky?" The word used most frequently in the accounts to describe the disappearance of Jesus is "taken", Jesus was "taken" from them. Whatever happened, that was the nearest and best word they could find.

## 6. Jesus Ascends into Heaven

### i.

#### John

Sensible men,
men with their feet
planted on the ground,
who are, they say, objective,
not given to dallying
in a fool's paradise,
not influenced by shades
or the gossamer world of dreams,
substantial men,
who recognize what is tangible,
solid, concrete, palpable,
such men

would be dismayed to learn
that the only reality is spirit.

The spirit *was*
before matter existed.
The spirit *is*
while matter decays.
The spirit *will be*
when every part of matter
has become dust
scattered by the wind of the spirit,
or reshaped by the design of his breath.
Without the spirit
matter has no meaning.
Without the spirit
there is no meaning.
We would be dismayed to learn,
if we had devoted our lives
to accumulating matter,
hoarding material things,
burying them in the ground,
hiding them, protecting them
in buildings of labyrinthine complexity
such as pleased the Pharaohs,
we would be, undoubtedly,
dismayed to find
that we had devoted ourselves
to the dross of existence.

We preach what is nonsense
to the sensible man,
impossible to the rational mind.
We preach Jesus Christ,
who, for love of us,
lived, suffered, was crucified
and rose from the dead,
who is Lord of life and death,

121

time and space,
matter and spirit.
And we who knew him
in Galilee and Judaea,
sometimes witnessed, without understanding,
moments when there seemed to be
a confusion between matter and spirit.
Moments when his reality astonished us.
And we flounder when we look for words
to describe what no human eye
has ever seen.
Such as the day we call
the day of his Ascension.
Ancient witnesses
to the transience of men,
mountains,
in all their rugged grandeur,
look with timeless patience
on the arrogance
of the dwarf-like creatures
strutting in their valleys
and on the plain.
Companions of the clouds,
wrapped in mystery,
they keep secrets
beyond our reach.

The feet of Jesus
consecrated
the Galilean hills,
his presence
sanctified their stones,
his prayers
hallowed their peaks.
He lived in their shadow,
preached on their slopes,
and alone with them

kept his vigils,
his assignations with the Father.

Where else
could his final tryst be kept,
the culmination of his mission,
save the summit of a mountain
from whose village
Lazarus was summoned from the dead;
a mountain
that overlooked the garden of his agony,
the city of his Passion,
the place of his resurrection;
where else, but
the Mount of Olives?

East of Jerusalem
the mountain stands,
taller than all its eastern brothers,
shading the western path
from the light of the rising sun.

From Bethany we came,
with the city across the valley
stirring in the warmth
of the waking day.

The chill of the shadows
slipped from us
as we emerged into the light.
And there he stood,
golden in the sun.

He waited
as we struggled,
winded from the climb,
Peter, James, Andrew and Philip,

Thomas, Matthew and Bartholomew,
James, son of Alphaeus,
Simon the Zealot,
Judas, son of James,
and me.

Then someone said,
"Lord, is it now
that you will restore the kingdom
to Israel?"
And he smiled,
for his Kingship and Kingdom
was established,
and the wind and the sky
and the sun in his might
awaited his command.
Then he commissioned us,
heralds of his word.
"You will receive power
when the Holy Spirit
has come upon you;
and you shall be my witnesses
in Jerusalem
and in all Judaea and Samaria
and to the end of the earth."

And the sun seemed to flare,
as if a mist had cleared his face,
lighting the clouds, blinding white,
as white as when he was transfigured.
And was he lifted up?
Or did the very mountain shrink beneath his feet,
humbled by his magnificence?
And did those dazzling clouds enfold him
in splendour beyond imagining.
The King of Kings
ascending his throne?

## THE STATIONS BEYOND THE CROSS

Whatever we saw
our eyes were filled with glory
and our ears with silent hallelujahs
harmonizing, mingling with his words –
You – Hallelujah! –
you shall be my witnesses –
my witnesses –
to the end of the earth,
Hallelujah!
Hallelujah!
Hallelujah!

ii.

*Risen, Ascended Lord,*
*I come before you*
*asking nothing save the happiness*
*of praising the triumph of your love.*
*Transform my gratitude*
*into a hymn of adoration.*
*May I always be filled*
*with the wonder of your being.*
*May I worship you,*
*with the skill of my hands,*
*with the thoughts of my mind,*
*with the words of my mouth,*
*with the days of my life.*
*May your love live in me*
*to the glory of your name.*

In this final "Station Beyond the Cross" we are dealing, yet again, with an event that words fail to capture. How do you describe a "spiritual" experience? It seemed to them that there was a sound, like a mighty wind – but nothing was blown down. They saw what looked like tongues of fire touching people's heads, but no one was burned. It is interesting to note that various people have, down the centuries, described spiritual experiences in similar words. John Wesley described the moment of his conversion in these words: "I felt my heart *strangely warmed.*" Richard Wurmbrand describes a moment of awareness of the presence of God, in a prison cell, by saying that he felt a *warm glow.*

The next thing that happens is nothing less than the complete reversal of the Tower of Babel story – one person speaks and people from fifteen different countries hear what is being said in their own language. Perhaps it was some form of mass spiritual experience. In some ways it seems to echo the thoughts of Paul when he said that the Holy Spirit speaks and interprets our prayers, thoughts and agonising in groans, "too deep for words".

## 7. The Disciples Receive the Holy Spirit

i.

*Peter*

It isn't easy to recapture
the waiting time.
Children remember their birthdays
and days of festive celebration,
but they forget the restlessness
of the night before,

the edgy excitement
that turns minutes into hours.
They forget the prickly, unscratchable itch
deep inside, that makes waiting
so excruciatingly unbearable.
You could say that like children
we were restive, fidgety,
on edge with expectancy,
and not a little apprehensive.
Truly, we were both eager and afraid.
We longed for the time to pass.
He had said, "Before many days",
but no one knew how many.

We had chosen Matthias
to make up the twelve,
a disciple from the beginning,
from John's baptism
to this very day,
and a witness to the resurrection.
So he waited with us
in the upper room,
fingers tapping,
no less impatient
for the coming of the Paraclete.

When it came it was sudden.
A roar of wind so loud
speech was wasted effort.
But our eyes spoke our terror
as we realized the sound
was within, not outside the room!
The walls were bathed in such a glow
as if a fire raged.
And then we saw the flames,
at least they looked like flames,
like tongues of fire

dancing on our heads!
And then, gone.
As if recalled
by a finger-snap.

And we began to speak
in other tongues,
not a babble,
but a flow of words,
in languages we did not know
yet understood!

The sound had roused the people
and they clamoured in the street.
People of every nation –
Parthians and Medes,
travellers from Mesopotamia,
from Egypt and Asia.
Visitors from Rome,
Greeks, Jews and Arabs,
and all understood!

And me, Simon Peter,
the horny-handed Galilean,
more at home hauling nets
than standing in a pulpit,
me, the fisherman from Bethsaida,
began to preach, with such power!
From the Psalms and from David
I declared our crucified Christ
Lord and King!
I told them they had heard
the sound of the breath of God.
I called them to repent,
to be baptized,
to beg the forgiveness of Christ
and to receive the gift

of the Holy Spirit.
And that day,
beginning in that hour,
in the name of the Father,
and of his son Jesus Christ,
and of the Holy Spirit,
there were baptized
three thousand souls.

The deed, at last, fitted the word
spoken by a total stranger,
who called to us as we worked
in our boats on the beach,
the first words I ever heard him speak,
"Follow me,
and I will make you fishers of men."


ii.


*Holy Spirit,*
*comforter, advocate, friend and guide,*
*I am not worthy*
*that you should live in me,*
*but in the name of Jesus,*
*my risen Lord,*
*I dare to ask for your power*
*in my life.*

*Holy Spirit,*
*let me hold open*
*the door of my soul*
*that your strength may enter*
*and transform my being;*
*that through you,*
*Christ my Lord*
*might live in me,*

*that through my hands,*
*through my voice,*
*through my life,*
*the world may know*
*how much the Father loves.*

*Merciful Father,*
*accept my praise and thanksgiving;*
*through your love*
*I am, by the Passion of Christ,*
*redeemed from sin,*
*by his resurrection,*
*released from death,*
*and by your Holy Spirit,*
*restored to life.*

# Bibliography

Aulen, Gustaf, *The Faith of the Christian Church*, S.C.M. Press.

Baillie, D.M., *God was in Christ*, Faber.

Barth, Karl, *Call for God*, S.C.M. Press.

Caird, G.B., *St Luke – A Pelican New Testament Commentary*, Penguin Books.

Cross, F.L., *The Oxford Dictionary of the Christian Church*, Oxford University Press.

Cupitt, Don, *Jesus and the Gospel of God*, Lutterworth Press.

Fenton, J.C., *St Matthew – A Pelican New Testament Commentary*, Penguin Books.

Goodier, Archbishop Alban, *The Passion and Death of Our Lord Jesus Christ*, Burns and Oates.

Marsh, John, *St John – A Pelican New Testament Commentary*, Penguin Books.

Moreton, H.V., *In the Steps of the Master*, Rich and Cowan.

Nineham, D.E., *St Mark – A Pelican New Testament Commentary*, Penguin Books.

Peake, A.S., *A Commentary on the Bible*, Thomas Nelson and Sons Ltd.

Richardson, Alan, *An Introduction to the Theology of the New Testament*, S.C.M. Press.

Richardson, Alan, *A Theological Word Book of the Bible*, S.C.M. Press.

Richardson, Alan, *Creeds in the Making*, S.C.M. Press.

Sanders, J.N. and Mastin, B.A., *A Commentary on the Gospel of St John*, A. and C. Black.

Vermes, Geza, *Jesus the Jew*, S.C.M. Press.

Vermes, Geza, *The Dead Sea Scrolls in English*, Pelican.

131

Wiles, Maurice, *Faith and the Mystery of God*, S.C.M. Press.

Williams, H.A., *The True Wilderness*, Constable, Fount Paperbacks.

Williams, H.A., *The True Resurrection*, Mitchell Beazley, Fount Paperbacks.

Wilson, Edward, *The Dead Sea Scrolls 1947–1969*, Fount Paperbacks.